First World War
and Army of Occupation
War Diary
France, Belgium and Germany

3 DIVISION
Divisional Troops
King's Royal Rifle Corps
20th Battalion Pioneers
27 March 1916 - 31 December 1916

WO95/1405/4

Published by

The Naval & Military Press Ltd

Unit 10 Ridgewood Industrial Park,

Uckfield, East Sussex,

TN22 5QE England

Tel: +44 (0) 1825 749494

www.naval-military-press.com

www.nmarchive.com

This diary has been reprinted in facsimile from the original. Any imperfections are inevitably reproduced and the quality may fall short of modern type and cartographic standards.

© **Crown Copyright**
Images reproduced by permission of The National Archives, London, England, 2015.

Contents

Document type	Place/Title	Date From	Date To
Heading	WO95/1405/4		
Heading	3rd Division Divl. Troops 20th Battalion K.R.R.C. Mar-Dec 1916.		
Heading	3rd Div Troops Box 1085 War Diary of 20th (S) Battn Kings Royal Rifle Corps (Pioneer) From 27th March 1916 To 30th April 1916 (Volume 1)		
War Diary	Southampton	27/03/1916	29/03/1916
War Diary	Havre	30/03/1916	30/03/1916
War Diary	Poperinghe	31/03/1916	02/04/1916
War Diary	A, 30 Central	03/04/1916	15/04/1916
War Diary	J Camp	16/04/1916	16/04/1916
War Diary	J, 17, a	17/04/1916	30/04/1916
Heading	Vol 1 20th Bn K R R C 27-3-16 To 30-4-16		
War Diary	Southampton	27/03/1916	29/03/1916
War Diary	Havre	30/03/1916	30/03/1916
War Diary	Poperinghe	31/03/1916	02/04/1916
War Diary	A 30 Central	03/04/1916	03/04/1916
War Diary	Oosthoek A 30 Central	04/04/1916	04/04/1916
War Diary	A 30 Central	05/04/1916	15/04/1916
War Diary	J Camp Poperinghe	16/04/1916	16/04/1916
War Diary	J 17, a, Winnezeele	17/04/1916	30/04/1916
Miscellaneous	20th Battalion, The King's Royal Rifle Corps. Appendix.		
Miscellaneous	Appendix 2		
Miscellaneous	Appendix 3		
Miscellaneous	Appendix 4		
Miscellaneous	Appendix 5		
Miscellaneous	Appendix 6		
Miscellaneous	Appendix 7		
Miscellaneous	Appendix 8		
Miscellaneous	Appendix 9		
Miscellaneous	20th Battalion. The King's Royal Rifle Corps. Appendix		
Miscellaneous	Appendix.		
Miscellaneous	Appendix 3		
Miscellaneous	Appendix 4		
Miscellaneous	Appendix 5		
Miscellaneous	Appendix 6		
Miscellaneous	Appendix 7		
Miscellaneous	Appendix 8		
Miscellaneous	Appendix 9		
Miscellaneous	20th Battalion. The King's Royal Rifle Corps. Appendix		
Miscellaneous	Appendix 2		
Miscellaneous	Appendix 3		
Miscellaneous	Appendix 4		
Miscellaneous	Appendix 5		
Miscellaneous	Appendix 6		
Miscellaneous	Appendix 7		
Miscellaneous	Appendix 8		
Miscellaneous	Appendix 9		

Heading	War Diary of 20th Bn Kings Royal Rifle Corps, (B.E.L. Pioneers) From 1st May 1916 To 31st May 1916 (Volume 2)		
War Diary	J. 17, a.	01/05/1916	09/05/1916
War Diary	A,9, B 8,2	10/05/1916	18/05/1916
War Diary	M,17,b,6,4	19/05/1916	23/05/1916
War Diary	M,6,d,	24/05/1916	31/05/1916
Heading	War Diary of 20th Bn Kings Royal Corps, (B.E.L. Pioneers) From 1st June 1916 To 30th June 1916 Volume 3.		
War Diary	M,6,d,	01/06/1916	30/06/1916
Heading	Pioneers. 3rd Div. War Diary 20th Battn. The King's Royal Rifle Corps. July 1916		
War Diary	M,6,d,	01/07/1916	07/07/1916
War Diary	A,14,a	08/07/1916	25/07/1916
War Diary	K,2,d,6,3	25/07/1916	29/07/1916
War Diary	J,5,a,8,8	30/07/1916	31/07/1916
Heading	3rd Divisional Troops 20th Battalion King's Royal Rifle Corps (Pioneers) August 1916		
Heading	War Diary for Period 1st To 31st August 1916		
War Diary	J,5,a,8,8	01/08/1916	11/08/1916
War Diary	F,13,b,9,9	12/08/1916	13/08/1916
War Diary	F,16,c,5,2	14/08/1916	21/08/1916
War Diary	Morlancourt	22/08/1916	23/08/1916
War Diary	Heuzecourt	24/08/1916	25/08/1916
War Diary	Frohen Le Grand	25/08/1916	26/08/1916
War Diary	Boubers Sur Canche	26/08/1916	26/08/1916
War Diary	Flammermont	26/08/1916	26/08/1916
War Diary	Monchy Cayeux	27/08/1916	27/08/1916
War Diary	Marest	28/08/1916	28/08/1916
War Diary	Houchin	29/08/1916	30/08/1916
War Diary	Philosophe	31/08/1916	31/08/1916
Heading	War Diary of 20th Bn. Kings Royal Rifle Corps, (B.E.L. Pioneers) From 1st September 1916 To 30th September 1916 Volume VI		
War Diary	Philosophe	01/09/1916	02/09/1916
War Diary	Mazingarbe	03/09/1916	23/09/1916
War Diary	Burbure	23/09/1916	23/09/1916
War Diary	Enguinegatte	24/09/1916	30/09/1916
Heading	Vol 7 War Diary 20th (S) Battalion KRR Corps (Pioneers) 1st To 31st October 1916		
War Diary	Enguinegatte	01/10/1916	04/10/1916
War Diary	Monchy Cayeux	05/10/1916	06/10/1916
War Diary	St Pol	07/10/1916	07/10/1916
War Diary	Beaussart	09/10/1916	09/10/1916
War Diary	Mailly Maillet	09/10/1916	19/10/1916
War Diary	P.6.Central (map. France 57. D)	20/10/1916	21/10/1916
War Diary	P.6 Central	23/10/1916	28/10/1916
War Diary	Courcelles	29/10/1916	31/10/1916
Miscellaneous	Officer i/c Adjutant General's Office At The Base.		
War Diary	Courcelles	01/11/1916	30/11/1916
Heading	War Diary of 20th (S) Battn King's Royal Rifle Corps (Pioneers) From 1st December 1916 To 31st December 1916 Volume IX		
War Diary	Courcelles	01/12/1916	31/12/1916

Heading   3rd Division 76th Inf. Bde 1917 B.H.Q. 2nd Suffolks. 8th K.O.Roy. Lancs 10th R.Welch Fus. 1st Gordon HRS. 76th Machine Gun Coy.

WO 95
14051/4

3RD DIVISION
DIVL. TROOPS

20TH BATTALION
K. R. R. C.
MAR-DEC 1916.

From UK

Confidential

2nd Div Troops

Box 1085

War Diary
of
20th (S) Battn. King's Royal Rifle Corps (Pioneers)

from 27th March 1916 to 20th April 1916.

(Volume 1)

XIV CORPS

WAR DIARY or INTELLIGENCE SUMMARY

Army Form C. 2118.

(Erase heading not required.)

Place	Date	Hour	Summary of Events and Information	Remarks and references to Appendices
Southampton	27/3/16	11 P.M.	The 20th (S) Battalion K.R.R.C. (B.E.L. Pioneers) left WELLINGBORO' in three trains at 7.15 a.m. 9.0 a.m. and 10.20 a.m. respectively, arriving at SOUTHAMPTON at 2.30 p.m. 4.0 P.M. and 5.0 P.M. The Battalion Zembarked on two (2) ships: 10 officers 212 other ranks and transport on the ROSSETTI, and 18 officers 772 other ranks on the MARGUERITTE. The MAR- GUERETTE sailed. The ROSSETTI attempted the voyage, but received orders to return and anchor in the SOLENT owing to bad weather.	
Southampton	28/3/16	11 P.M.	The ROSSETTI remained at anchor till 4.30 P.M. meanwhile the MARGUERETTE returned to SOUTHAMPTON at 12 noon, having suffered considerably from heavy seas. The 18 officers and 772 other ranks proceeded to the Rest Camp at SOUTHAMPTON for the night. The ROSSETTI made another attempt to sail, but returned once more to the SOLENT and anchored for the night.	
Southampton	29/3/16	11 P.M.	The ROSSETTI left for HAVRE at 4.30 P.M. The remainder of the Battalion remained at the SOUTHAMPTON Rest Camp	
Havre	30/3/16	12 P.M.	The ROSSETTI reached HAVRE at 4 A.M. At 7 A.M. all ranks and transport were disembarked with orders to remain at HAVRE dock until 8 P.M. when party marched to entrain at GARE DE MARCHANDISE. The train left HAVRE at 11.55 P.M. The remainder of the Battalion at SOUTHAMPTON sailed for HAVRE at 6 P.M. on S.S. KING EDWARD	

WAR DIARY or INTELLIGENCE SUMMARY

Army Form C. 2118.

(Erase heading not required.)

Place	Date	Hour	Summary of Events and Information	Remarks and references to Appendices
Poperinghe	31/3/16	12 P.M.	The 11.55 P.M. from HAVRE reached HAZEBROUCK at 5 P.M.) tender orders were received to proceed to POPERINGHE which place was reached at 8 P.M. After detrainment the Party (600 Transport were mustered with guide to "D" Camp, 20th Division). The transport being led by another guide to their quarters. The S.S. KING EDWARD reached HAVRE at 6.30 A.M. after discharging its party proceeded to HAVRE Rest Camp, eventually entraining for ROUEN at 11.30 P.M. The Commanding Officer reported to 20th D.H.Q. at 6 A.M. and received instructions as to areas of work for Companies.	
Poperinghe	1/4/16	8 P.M.	9.30 A.M. The second party reached ROUEN at 8.30 P.M. while it was entrained for POPERINGHE to report at C.20 nearly awake at 2 A.M., 2 officers left Camp to reconnoitre area of work. The second party arrived at POPERINGHE at 5.30 P.M. and marched to "D" Camp, 20th Division. 1 Company left to work at C.20, nearly central at 6 P.M. but returned owing to there being no train arranged for, as promised.	
Poperinghe	2/4/16	8 P.M.		

WAR DIARY or INTELLIGENCE SUMMARY

Army Form C. 2118.

Place	Date	Hour	Summary of Events and Information	Remarks and references to Appendices
A 30 central.	3/4/16	12 P.M.	One company left at 6 P.M. to work on drainage of trenches at C,20,d,3,5. Officers left during the day to reconnoitre areas for work at C,13, about central; and B,12,d,8,6,2; B,18, about central; and C,22,d,6,4, respectively.	
A 30 Central.	4/4/16	12 AM	One Company worked on drainage of trenches Sat C,20,d,3,5.	
A 30 Central.	5/4/16	12 AM	One Company started draining and repairing of parapets at C,13, about central; another Company cleared & choked up stream at C,20,b,3,6, and drained a trench at C,20,c,3,2½. Another worked on communication trench leading to a machine gun emplacement, converted a subterranean safe hole into an observation post, made a new cutting 35 feet long and made an observation post at B,12,d,8,8; materials for work for the following night were carried from the dumps to B,18, about central. Approximately 150 yards of tram line were levelled off at B,22,d,6,3, and 250 sleepers were laid and covered from view of enemy aircraft.	

Army Form C. 2118.

WAR DIARY
or
INTELLIGENCE SUMMARY

(Erase heading not required.)

Instructions regarding War Diaries and Intelligence Summaries are contained in F. S. Regs., Part II. and the Staff Manual respectively. Title Pages will be prepared in manuscript.

Place	Date	Hour	Summary of Events and Information	Remarks and references to Appendices
A,30, Central	6/4/16	12 AM	About 250 yards of drainage trench were cleared at C,20,b,3,7, and communication trench at C,20,c,3,2½, was occupied in draining. Another Company was occupied in draining, sandbagging, repairing of parapets of communication trench C,13, about central. Further materials for work were carried from dump F,3,B, about central, where about 20 yards of wiring were completed by the remaining Company.	
A,30, Central	7/4/16	12 AM	One Company carried out revetting work at C,20,c,3,2½. trench clearing at C,20,b,3,7; and started a communication trench at C,20,b,3,7. One man was killed, and one slightly wounded. Another Company carried on draining, sandbagging, and repairing of parapet at C,13, about central. The remaining Company carried on construction of tram line at B,22,d,6,3, ground-levelling, and sleeper-laying comprised the nights work.	
A,30, Central	8/4/16	12 AM	One Company continued digging trench (communication) at C,20,b,3,7; Draining of communication trench at C,20,C,3,2½, was also continued, and improvements at C,20,b,3,7, were carried on.	

Army Form C. 2118.

WAR DIARY
or
INTELLIGENCE SUMMARY

(Erase heading not required.)

Place	Date	Hour	Summary of Events and Information	Remarks and references to Appendices
A 30, Central	8/4/16	12 AM	At C,13, about central, cleaning and revetting of a trench was carried out by one company, which also employed a number of men in carrying sails, trench bombs etc; and wire gabions and U frames were conveyed to canal bridge at C,13, e, 2, 3. Another company at B, 12, d, 8, 7, heightened with sandbags a communication trench leading to the bays and improved wall. (A new communication trench would change in its alignment etc) The same company cleaned obstruction from parapet & deepened a levelled floor so far as hostile m.g. fire in the subterranean parapet could let be continued. In front were emplacements at B, 18, about central, 40 yards of wiring were camouflaged (partly while at B, 22, d, 6, 3) rails & sleepers were also carried out, and to laying; cutting & levelling for track was done as well. The remaining company continued draining communication trench at C, 20, b, 3, 7, A trench at C, 20, b, 3, 7, was revetted, while revetting work was carried on at C, 20, C, 3, 2½.	

2449 Wt. W14957/M90 750,000 1/16 J.B.C. & A. Forms/C.2118/12.

WAR DIARY or INTELLIGENCE SUMMARY

Army Form C. 2118.

Place	Date	Hour	Summary of Events and Information	Remarks and references to Appendices
A.30, central	9/1/16	12 AM	One Company carried out revetting and construction of parapet and drainage at C.20, a, 3, 2, and moved U frames and corrugated iron from C.19, c, 5, 0, to C.20, d, 3, 7, where a trench was erected. Another company at C.13, about central, conveyed stores to work from C.13, d, 3, 2, 2, to C.13, about central, drained a communication trench and filled sandbags and made use of same at C.13, about central. Another company fixed a pump in sap head at B.12, d, 8, 7, but unsatisfactory flow was made on account of pump not acting well. The trench in the traymore (tramway) electrified and behind was blown up to thicken parapet. No parapet of a communication trench has been built up with sandbags and filled in behind with earth. A trench which had been pushed in by an aerial torpedo was partially cleared out, and part of a bombing trench was straightened and deepened. All this took place at B.12, d, 8, 7. At B.18, about central, 50 yards of barbed wire entanglements were erected, & stakes taken from the dump. At B.22, d, 6, 3, about 200 yards of sleepers and rails were laid and baulks	

WAR DIARY
or
INTELLIGENCE SUMMARY
(Erase heading not required.)

Army Form C. 2118.

Place	Date	Hour	Summary of Events and Information	Remarks and references to Appendices
A.30, Central	10/4/16	12 AM	One company completed repairs to M.G. saps, revetted communication trench walls by means of sandbags and finished cutting for bombing trench at B,12, d, 8, 7. While at B,18, about central, 50 more yards of wire entanglement were erected. Pickets were driven in two a distance of 50 yards and a start was made for laying 2 new traverses. At B,22,d,6,3, work continues with the carrying of rails & sleepers, packing along men continues to the carrying of rails & sleepers, packing along tram line. Another company at C,13, about central, carried on repairs & drainage of communication trench and continued to repair parapets & field sandbags. 3 men were wounded. The remaining Company carried on improvement of parapet at E,20, c, 3, 2½ and continued work on communication trench C,20, b, 3, 7.	
A,30, Central	11/4/16	12 AM	One company at B,12,d,8,7, carried out sandbag revetting to 2 communication trenches, worked on cutting for bombing straight, and humped M.G. sap. At B,18, about central, 50 yards of wire was completed, sandbags were filled and traverse built & wired in trench X. At B,22,d,6,3, line were built. At B,22,d,6,3, rails & sleepers and packing for tram line were carried up to work.	

Army Form C. 2118.

WAR DIARY
or
INTELLIGENCE SUMMARY
(Erase heading not required.)

Instructions regarding War Diaries and Intelligence Summaries are contained in F. S. Regs., Part II. and the Staff Manual respectively. Title Pages will be prepared in manuscript.

Place	Date	Hour	Summary of Events and Information	Remarks and references to Appendices
A.30, central	11/4/16	12 AM	Another Company worked on drainage and general repair work of communication trench at C,13, about central; one man, a sergeant, was wounded in the shoulder on leaving work. The remaining Company filled sandbags, revetted and built up parapet of trench L at C,20, c, 3, 2, 3, while at C,20, b, 3, 7, the new communication trench was revetted and a further extension of the trench was planned and started. One man, a Lance Corporal, was wounded.	
A.30, central	12/4/16	12 AM	Owing to the development of an attack on the enemy between the hours of 6 and 9 P.M. only one Company was able to proceed with its work. Material for work was carried from dump to C,20, c, 3, 2½ and C,20, b, 3, 7.	
A.30, central	13/4/16	12 AM	One Company worked on tram line at B,22, d, 6, 3, while at B,12, d, 8, 7, hurdles, pickets, wire, mauls, & sandbags, were carried up to the trenches, 6 hurdles being put into bombing trench, and part of the bombing trench being deepened. At B,18, about central, sand bags were thrown up, and the trench was cleared and traverses rebuilt. One man was killed. At B,29,a, a trench 400 yards long was dug and a cable laid in it at a depth of 2 ft 6 ins and about 5	

Army Form C. 2118.

WAR DIARY
or
INTELLIGENCE SUMMARY
(Erase heading not required.)

Instructions regarding War Diaries and Intelligence Summaries are contained in F. S. Regs., Part II. and the Staff Manual respectively. Title Pages will be prepared in manuscript.

Place	Date	Hour	Summary of Events and Information	Remarks and references to Appendices
A.30, Central	13/4/16	12 A.M.	Another company revetted and strengthened 100 feet of parapet at C,20,c,3,2½, while 80 yards of new trench was deepened at C,20,b,3,7, where in addition to this work, 30 yards of new trench was dug, and communication trench was drained. The remaining Company carried material to trench at C,13. About central, sheet draining and repairing of the parapet was carried out, and wire revetting and sand bagging was done.	
A.30, Central	14/4/16	12 A.M.	Two drainage trenches were cleared by one company at C,20, about central, while sand bags were filled, and the parapet thickened at trench at C,20, c, 3, 2 ½. Another Company drained and repaired generally the communication trench at C,13, about central. One man was wounded while engaged in filling sandbags. The remaining Company continued sand bag revetting or bombing shaft revetting at B,12,d,8,7, while wiring and sand-bag revetting was carried on at B,18, about central, 21 men of the Party being engaged in carrying material to M.G. emplacement from B,17,d,8,2,3, and at B,22,d,6,3. Packing of new line was completed, and siding for engine house was started.	

WAR DIARY
or
INTELLIGENCE SUMMARY

Army Form C. 2118.

Place	Date	Hour	Summary of Events and Information	Remarks and references to Appendices
A 30 Central	15/4/16	8 P.M.	Sand-bagging and revetting was continued on the Communication trench by one Company at C.13, about one turn, and the morning. Revetted a trench with sand-bags & propped out water and repaired a bombing branch trench while at C.13. Carrying up trench mortars at B.12, d.1, 87, while at B.18, about 500 (?) mortar was carried up from Ramon Dump and several boxes of S.A.A. Carrying for M.G. emplacements was done out from B.17, d.8,2. The same Company also repaired trench at B.17, d.8,2. The sand bagged side at B.22, M.613. Packing an engine bed, and the line was done out from B.15, Carnoy St. Tramway beyond the line was done while waiting Carrying Bodies with rails & material were continued. Carrying to Packed Generals was continued from Carnoy Side of Tramway to C.20,a.3,2,6. The remaining Company worked on trench Bouquet about central and continued working to C.19, about central. The battalion marched out from A.30 Central at 10.35 A.M. arrived with field kitchens at J Camp about former about 4.30 P.M.	
J Camp	16/4/16	6 P.M.	The battalion and all transport arrived (?) at 8.17 a.m. and were in billets by 6 P.M.	

Army Form C. 2118.

WAR DIARY
or
INTELLIGENCE SUMMARY
(Erase heading not required.)

Instructions regarding War Diaries and Intelligence Summaries are contained in F.S. Regs., Part II. and the Staff Manual respectively. Title Pages will be prepared in manuscript.

Place	Date	Hour	Summary of Events and Information	Remarks and references to Appendices
J.17.a.	17/4/16	8 P.M.	The battalion commenced training according to scheme of work submitted to D.H.Q.— (Platoon & squad drill; and musketry). The latter being rendered difficult owing to entire absence of musketry instruction appliances, and to the battalion borrowing only 1230 rifles. These were obtained on instructions from D.H.Q. Unfortunately, this total was all that could be found, which fact strongly emphasises the need for a plentiful supply of arms (to be available for divisional & other losses). The somewhat exceptional circumstances under which the unit arrived at a danger zone to work, should have influenced the home authorities to see that rifles were provided for the battalion on its arrival at such a destination.	
J.17.a.	18/4/16	8 P.M.	Training in the Squad & platoon drill and musketry continued.	
J.17.a.	19/4/16	8 P.M.	→ Training in squad drill, extended order drill, & musketry.	
J.17.a.	20/4/16	8 P.M.	→ The usual instruction carried out.	
J.17.a.	21/4/16	8 P.M.	→ Training was carried on during morning only.	
J.17.a.	22/4/16	8 P.M.	→ Morning programme carried out.	

Army Form C. 2118.

WAR DIARY
or
INTELLIGENCE SUMMARY
(Erase heading not required.)

Instructions regarding War Diaries and Intelligence Summaries are contained in F. S. Regs., Part II. and the Staff Manual respectively. Title Pages will be prepared in manuscript.

Place	Date	Hour	Summary of Events and Information	Remarks and references to Appendices
J.17.a	23/4/16	8 P.M.	Sunday observed as day of rest.	
J.17.a	24/4/16	8 P.M.	Pioneer training commenced in earnest. R.E. Fm. run. Two Companies employed in digging fire trench and Maple trench. Remainder continue training in musketry, bomb-throwing, bayonet fighting, wire entanglements, pioneering, and musketry as in former day.	
J.17.a	25/4/16	8 P.M.		
J.17.a	26/4/16	8 P.M.	Sand-bagging revetting wiring [illegible] instruction. One N.C.O. and ten men at wing ends rifle range of 30 yards in disused farm house.	
J.17.a	27/4/16	8 P.M.	Trench digging and musketry training. One Company detailed to cut brushwood for making of fascines.	
J.17.a	28/4/16	8 P.M.	30 yard range completed with exception of targets. Musketry and trench digging and wiring continues. Fascine-making carried out so far during so far as two Companies.	

WAR DIARY
or
INTELLIGENCE SUMMARY
(Erase heading not required.)

Army Form C. 2118.

Place	Date	Hour	Summary of Events and Information	Remarks and references to Appendices
In a	29/4/16	8 P.M.	The Battalion marched by Companies to C.16.b. to get washed and to receive change of under-clothing. The four Companies received 500 dummy cartridges each. They also were issued with two dummy Vickers & Lewis guns. During the past week, instructed recruit drills and parades were employed in the housing & trade.	* Observations by C.O. on progress of 2 weeks training
4/17 a	30/4/16	8 P.M.	* The Battalion will command on the 1st of next month the final course (Table A) in the 30 yards range. The firing points have been purchased, sufficient white paper to make a stock of targets for the purpose of training received during this was the resting period for musketry weeks of the primitive arrangement. Instruction in spite of the adverse circumstances by the men and The intelligent & best Officers, & largely to the instruction imparted by can? tow furnished legacy to the rate & progress. The anyful suggestion & supervision of the ... Officers produced good work in trench digging up, parties, R.E. etc. Looking and general Pioneer work.	J. M.

Vol. I.
20th Bn KRRC

27-3-16

to

30-4-16

Army Form C. 2118

WAR DIARY
or
INTELLIGENCE SUMMARY.
(Erase heading not required.)

20th "B"
March (was 15)
1916 { April

Instructions regarding War Diaries and Intelligence Summaries are contained in F.S. Regs, Part II. and the Staff Manual respectively. Title pages will be prepared in manuscript.

Place	Date	Hour	Summary of Events and Information	Remarks and references to Appendices
SOUTHAMPTON	27.3.16	11 p.m.	The 20th (S) battalion K.R.R.C. (B.E. Stonnars) left Wellington's in three trains at 7.15 a.m., 9.0 a.m. and 10.20 a.m. respectively, arriving at SOUTHAMPTON at 2.30 p.m., 4 p.m., and 5 p.m. The Battalion embarked on two (2) ships: 10 Officers and 212 other ranks and transport on the ROSSETTI, and 18 Officers, 792 other ranks on the MARGUERETTE. The MARGUERETTE sailed; the ROSSETTI attempted the voyage, but received orders to return and anchor in the SOLENT owing to bad weather.	
SOUTHAMPTON	28.3.16	11 p.m.	The ROSSETTI remained at anchor till 4.30 p.m., meanwhile the MARGUERETTE returned to SOUTHAMPTON at 12 noon having suffered considerably from heavy seas. The 18 Officers and 792 other ranks he proceeded to the Rest Camp at SOUTHAMPTON for the night. The ROSSETTI made another attempt to sail, but returned once more to the SOLENT and anchored for the night.	
SOUTHAMPTON	29.3.16	11 p.m.	The ROSSETTI left for HAVRE at 4.30 p.m. The remainder of the Battalion remained at the SOUTHAMPTON Rest Camp.	
HAVRE	30.3.16	12 p.m.	The ROSSETTI reached HAVRE at 4 a.m. At 7 a.m. all ranks and transport were disembarked, with orders to remain at HAVRE dock until 8 p.m. when party marched to entrain at GARE DE MARCHANDISE. The train left HAVRE at 11.55 p.m. The remainder of the Battalion at SOUTHAMPTON sailed for HAVRE at 6 p.m. on S.S. KING EDWARD.	

WAR DIARY
INTELLIGENCE SUMMARY.
(Erase heading not required.)

Army Form C. 2118

Instructions regarding War Diaries and Intelligence Summaries are contained in F. S. Regs., Part II. and the Staff Manual respectively. Title pages will be prepared in manuscript.

Place	Date	Hour	Summary of Events and Information	Remarks and references to Appendices
POPERINGHE	31.3.16	12 P.M.	The 11.55 P.M. from HAVRE reached HAZEBROUCK at 5 P.M.; here, orders were received to proceed to POPERINGHE, which place was reached at 8 P.M. After detrainment the party less transport were marched with guide to "D"Camp 20th Division; the transport to be by another guide to their quarters. The S.S. KING EDWARD reached HAVRE at 6.30 P.M. After disembarking the party proceeded to HAVRE Rest Camp, eventually entraining for ROUEN at 11.30 P.M.	
POPERINGHE	1.4.16	8 P.M.	The Commanding Officer reported to 20th D.H.Q at 7.30 A.M. and received instructions as to areas of work for Companies. The second party reached ROUEN at 6 A.M. where it was entrained for POPERINGHE at 8.30 P.M.	
POPERINGHE	2.4.16	8 P.M.	At 2 P.M., 2 Officers & 1 Coy: left to report at C.20. nearly Central to reconnoitre area of work. The second party arrived at POPERINGHE at 5.30 P.M. and marched to D'Camp 20th DIVISION. 1 Company left for work at C.20, nearly central at 6 P.M. but returned owing to there being no train arranged for, as promised.	
A.30.Central	3.4.16	12 P.M.	One company left at 6 P.M. to work on drainage of trenches at C.20, d.3, 5. Officers left during the day to reconnoitre areas for work at C.13, about Centrals B,12, d, 8, 6.5; B,18, about Central; and C,22,d, b,4 respectively.	

Army Form C. 2118

WAR DIARY
INTELLIGENCE SUMMARY.
(Erase heading not required.)

Place	Date	Hour	Summary of Events and Information	Remarks and references to Appendices
OOSTHOEK				
A.30.Central	4.4.16	12 A.M.	One Company worked on drainage of trenches at C.20.d, 3, 5.	
A.30 Central	5.4.16	12 A.M.	One Company started draining and repairing of parapet at C.13, about Central; another Company cleared and choked up stream at C.20, C.3.7, cleaned a trench at C.25.6, 3, 6, and worked on communication trench at C.20, C.3, 2½. Another company improved a subterranean cap leading to a machine gun emplacement, constructed a shell hole into an observation post, made a new cutting 35 feet long, and made an observation post at B.12.d, 88. Materials for work for the following night were carried from the dump to B.18, about Central. Approximately 150 yards of tram line were laid off at B.22, d, b, 3, and 250 chevaux were laid and carried from view of enemy aircraft.	
A.30. Central	6.4.16	12 A.M.	About 250 yards of drainage trench was cleared at C.20, C.3.Y, and communication trench at C.20, C.3.2½ was drained by one Company. Another Company was employed in draining, sandbagging and repairing of parapets of communication trench C.13, about Central. Further materials for work were carried from dump to B.18 about Central, where about 20 yards of wiring were completed by the remaining Company.	

T2134. Wt. W708—776. 500000. 4/15. Sir J. C. & S.

Army Form C. 2118.

WAR DIARY
INTELLIGENCE SUMMARY
(Erase heading not required.)

Instructions regarding War Diaries and Intelligence Summaries are contained in F. S. Regs., Part II. and the Staff Manual respectively. Title Pages will be prepared in manuscript.

Place	Date	Hour	Summary of Events and Information	Remarks and references to Appendices
A.30.Central	7.4.16	12 A.M.	One Company carried out wiring was at C.20, c.3, 3, 2½; Trench was at C.20, b.3, Y; and started a communication trench at C.20, 2.3, Y. One man was killed and one slightly wounded. Another company carried on wiring, sandbagging and repairing of parapet at C.3, about Central. Was remaining company carried on construction of tram line at B.22, d, b.3, groundsheeting and duckboard-laying comprised the night's work.	
A.30.Central	8.4.16	12 A.M.	One Company continued digging trench (communication) at C.20, b.3, Y; drawing of communication trench at C.20, b.3, Y was also continued and wire-front at C.20, C, 3, 2½; were carried on.	
A.30.Central	8.4.16	12 A.M.	At C.13, about Central, cleaning and erecting of a trench was carried out by one company, which also employed a number of men in carrying sick bench boards, and wire gabions and U frames were arranged to bound bridge at C.13, C.2.3. Another Company at B.12, d, 6.7 Haig Reserve with wiredbags a communication trench leading to firestep, and improved wall thereof. A new communication trench was changed in its alignment and expanded. The same Company cleared obstruction from drainage and headless from as far as possible but the subterranean passage could not be continued as pump was out of order.	

2449 Wt. W14957/M90 750,000 1/16 J.B.C. & A. Forms/C.2118/12.

WAR DIARY

INTELLIGENCE SUMMARY

Army Form C. 2118.

Place	Date	Hour	Summary of Events and Information	Remarks and references to Appendices
A.30. Central	8.4.16	12A.m	At B,18, about Central, 40 yards of wiring were completed, while at B,22,d, 6,3, nails and sleepers were carried to positions for laying; cutting and levelling for track was also carried out and bankimg was done as well. The remaining Company continued draining Communication trench at C,20, 6,3,7. A trench at C,20, 6,3,7, was revetted, while revetting work was carried on at C,20, C,3, 2½.	
A.30. Central	9.4.16	12A.M.	One Company carried out revetting and construction of a parapet and drainage at C.20, C,3, 2½, and moved U frames and corrugated iron from C,19, C,5,0, to C,20, 6,3,7, where a trench was revetted. Another Company at C,13, about central, conveyed stores for work from C.13, 6,3,22, to C.13, about central; drained a communication trench and filled sandbags and made use of same at C.13, about central. Another company fixed a pump in sap head at B,12,d, 8,7, but unsatisfactory progress was made on account of pump not acting well. The trench in the bay was deepened, and earth was thrown up to thicken parapet. The parapet of a communication trench was built up with sandbags and filled in behind with earth. A trench which had been knocked in by an Aerial Torpedo was partially cleared out, and part of a bombing trench was straightened and deepened. All this took place at B,12,d, 6,7. At B,18, about Central, 50 yards of barbed wire entanglements were erected, and stakes taken from the front. At B,22,d, 6,3, about 200 yards of sleepers and nails were laid and banked.	

WAR DIARY
INTELLIGENCE SUMMARY
(Erase heading not required.)

Army Form C. 2118

Place	Date	Hour	Summary of Events and Information	Remarks and references to Appendices
B.30, Central	10.4.16	12 A.M.	One company completed repairs to M.G. Sap; revetted 2 communication trenches by means of sandbags, and finished cutting for bombing trench at B,12,b,8,y. Whilst at B,18, about Central, 50 yards of wire entanglements were erected, trenches were driven in for a distance of 50 yards, and a start was made for laying two new traverses. At B,22,d, b,3, men continued with carrying of rails and sleepers, and packing along tram line. Another Company at C,13, about Central, carried on repairs and drainage of communication trench, and continued to repair parapets and fill sandbags. 3 men were wounded. The remaining Company carried on improvement of parapet at C.10, b,3,y.	
B.30, Central	11.4.16	12 A.M.	One company at B,12,d,8,y, carried out sandbag revetting to 2 communication trenches, worked on cutting for bombing straight, and pumped M.G. Sap. At B,18, about Central, 50 yards of wiring was completed, sandbags were filled, and traverses and fire trench in New X line were built. At B,22,d, b,3, rails, sleepers, and packing for tram line were carried up for work. Another company worked on drainage and general repair work of communication trench at C,13, about central; one man, a sergeant was wounded on shoulder on leaving work.	

Army Form C. 2118.

WAR DIARY
INTELLIGENCE SUMMARY.
(Erase heading not required.)

Instructions regarding War Diaries and Intelligence Summaries are contained in F.S. Regs., Part II. and the Staff Manual respectively. Title pages will be prepared in manuscript.

Place	Date	Hour	Summary of Events and Information	Remarks and references to Appendices
A30, Central	11.4.16	12 A.M.	The remaining Company filled sandbags, revetted, and built up parapet of trench at C.20, c.3,2½, while at C.20, b.3,7, the new communication trench was revetted, and a further extension of the trench was planned and started. One man, a Lance Corporal was wounded.	
A30, Central	12.4.16	12 A.M.	Owing to the development of an attack on the part of the enemy between the hours of 6 and 9 p.m. only one Company was able to proceed with its work. Material for work was carried from dumps to C.20, c.3,2½, and C.20, b.3,7.	
A30, Central	13.4.16	12 A.M.	One Company worked on tram line at B.2,2, d, 6,3 while at B,12,d,8,7, hurdles, pickets, wire, mauls & sandbags were carried up to the trenches, 8 hurdles being put into bombing trench and part of the bombing trench being deepened. At B,18, about central, sandbags were thrown up, and the trench was cleared and traverse rebuilt. One man was killed. At B.29, a, a trench 400 yards long was dug and a cable laid in it at a depth of 2ft 6ins and buried. Another company revetted and strengthened 100 feet of parapet at C.20, b.3,7, while 80 yards of new trench was deepened at C.20, b.3,7, where in addition to this work, 30 yards of new trench was dug and communication trench was drained. The remaining Company carried material to trench at C.13, about Central, where traversing and repairing of the parapet was carried out, and wire revetting and sandbagging was done.	

T2134. Wt. W708-776. 500000. 4/15. Sir J. C. & B.

WAR DIARY
INTELLIGENCE SUMMARY.
(Erase heading not required.)

Army Form C. 2118.

Place	Date	Hour	Summary of Events and Information	Remarks and references to Appendices
A.30, Central	14.4.16	12 A.M.	Two drainage trenches were cleared by one Company at C.20 about Central, while sandbags were filled and the parapet thickened and repaired at C.20,c,3,2½. Another Company drained and repaired generally the communication trench at C.13 about central. One man was wounded while engaged in filling sandbags. The remaining Company continued and dug revetting in parting straight trench at B.18, d,6,3, while wiring and sandbag revetting was carried on at B.18, about Central, 21 men of this party being engaged in carrying material to M.G. emplacement from B.17, d, 8, 2; and at B.22, d, 6, 3. Packing of the line was completed, and wiring for engine house was started.	
A.30, Central	15.4.16	8 P.M.	Sandbagging and revetting was continued in the Communication trench by one company at C.13, about Central; another Company revetted a bench with sandbags, pumped out water, and repaired a bombing straight trench which had been blown up by trench mortars at B.12, d, 8, 4, while at B.18, about Central, material was carried up from Barrier Dump, and wiring was continued. Carrying from M.G. emplacement was carried out from B.17, d, 8, 2: the same Company also supplied labour on engine shed trench line at B.22, d, 6,3. Packing of tramway beyond junction was done, rails were carried & trollies with rail and material were dumped.	

WAR DIARY
INTELLIGENCE SUMMARY

Army Form C. 2118

Place	Date	Hour	Summary of Events and Information	Remarks and references to Appendices
A.30 Central	15.4.16	8 p.m.	Carrying and packing generally was continued from canal side of tramway. The remaining Company worked on French parapet at C.20, c, 3, 22, and continued working at C.20, about Central. The Battalion marched out from A.30, Central at 10.35 A.M., arriving with field Kitchens at "J" Camp about 4 p.m.	
"J" Camp	16.4.16	8 p.m.	The Battalion and all transport arrived about 4.30 p.m. at "J"17, a, and was in billets by 6 P.M.	
POPERINGHE "J" 17, a, WINNEZEELE	17.4.16	8 p.m.	The Battalion commenced training according to scheme of work submitted to D.H.Q. - (Platoon and squad drill and musketry) the latter being rendered difficult owing to the entire absence of musketry instruction appliances, and to the Battalion possessing only 230 rifles. There were obtained on instructions from D.H.Q. Unfortunately the total was all that could be spared, which fact strongly emphasises the need for a plentiful supply of arms to be available for divisional and other troops. The somewhat exceptional circumstances under which the unit arrived at a danger zone to work, should have influenced the home authorities to see that influence was provided for the Battalion on its arrival at such a destination.	

Army Form C. 2118.

WAR DIARY

~~INTELLIGENCE~~ SUMMARY.

(Erase heading not required.)

Instructions regarding War Diaries and Intelligence Summaries are contained in F. S. Regs., Part II. and the Staff Manual respectively. Title pages will be prepared in manuscript.

Place	Date	Hour	Summary of Events and Information	Remarks and references to Appendices
WINNEZEELE				
J.17.a.	18.4.16	8 P.M.	Training in squad and platoon drill and musketry continued.	
J.17.a.	19.4.16	8 P.M.	Training in squad drill, extended order drill & musketry	
J.17.a.	20.4.16	8 P.M.	The usual instruction carried out	
J.17.a.	21.4.16	8 P.M.	Training was carried on during morning only.	
J.17.a.	22.4.16	8 P.M.	Morning programme carried out	
J.17.a.	23.4.16	8 P.M.	Sunday observed as a day of rest.	
J.17.a.	24.4.16	8 P.M.	Pioneer training commenced in conjunction with R.E. Field Company. Two Companies employed in digging and revetting fire trench and traffic trench. Remaining two Companies continued training in Musketry, bombs, Lewis gun, platoon drill &c, to erect barbed wire entanglements.	
J.17.a.	25.4.16	8 P.M.	Bombing and musketry as on previous day.	
J.17.a.	26.4.16	8 P.M.	Sandbagging, revetting and wiring practice; musketry instruction. One N.C.O. and ten men detailed to erect range of 30 yards in disused farm house.	
J.17.a.	27.4.16	8 P.M.	Trench digging and musketry training. One officer and 50 men detailed to cut brush wood for making of fascines.	

Army Form C. 2118.

WAR DIARY
INTELLIGENCE SUMMARY.
(Erase heading not required.)

Instructions regarding War Diaries and Intelligence Summaries are contained in F. S. Regs., Part II. and the Staff Manual respectively. Title pages will be prepared in manuscript.

Place	Date	Hour	Summary of Events and Information	Remarks and references to Appendices
J.17.a.	28.4.16	8 a.m.	30 yards range completed with exception of targets. Musketry and trench digging and wiring was carried out as per training scheme. Favours making was commenced.	
J.17.a.	29.4.16	8 p.m.	The Battalion marched by companies to C.16 to get unclothed and to receive change of underclothing.	
J.17.a.	30.4.16	8 p.m.	The four Companies received 500 dummy cartridges each, they also were issued with two aiming tripods apiece. During the past week, improvised aiming discs and targets were employed in the training of men.	
			* The battalion will commence on the first of next month the firing course (Table A) on the 30 yard range, sufficient white paper having been purchased for the purpose of making a stock of targets.	* Observation by C.O. on progress of two weeks training
			The training received during the first two weeks of the resting period has been satisfactory in spite of rather primitive arrangements for musketry. The intelligent interest evinced by the men and the instruction imparted by Officers contribute largely to the rate of progress. The helpful suggestions and supervision of the R.E. Officers produced good work in trench digging, revetting, wiring and general pioneer work.	

T2134. Wt. W708—776. 500000. 4/15. Sir J. C. & S.

20th BATTALION, THE KING'S ROYAL RIFLE CORPS.

1916   Appendix.

March   SOUTHAMPTON.

27th 11 PM.   The 20th (S) Battalion, K.R.R.C. (B.E.L. Pioneers) left Wellingboro' in three trains at 7.15 a.m., 9.0 am, and 10.20 a.m. respectively, arriving at SOUTHAMPTON at 2.30 p.m., 4 p.m. and 5 p.m. The Battalion embarked on two (2) ships; 10 Officers 212 other ranks and Transport on the ROSSETTI, and 18 Officers, 772 other ranks on the MARGUERETTE.
The MARGUERETTE sailed; the ROSSETTI attempted the voyage, but received orders to return and anchor in the SOLENT owing to bad weather.

28th 11 PM   The ROSSETTI remained at anchor till 4.30 P.M., meanwhile the MARGUERETTE returned to SOUTHAMPTON at 12 noon having suffered considerably from heavy seas. The 18 Officers and 772 other ranks proceeded to the Rest Camp at SOUTHAMPTON for the night. The ROSSETTI made another attempt to sail, but returned once more to the SOLENT and anchored for the night.

29th 11 PM   The ROSSETTI left for HAVRE at 4.30 P.M. The remainder of the Battalion remained at the SOUTHAMPTON Rest Camp.

                 HAVRE.

30th 12 PM   The ROSSETTI reached HAVRE at 4 a.m. At 7 A.M. all ranks and Transport were disembarked, with orders to remain at HAVRE dock until 8 P.M. when party marched to entrain at GARE DE MARCHANDISE. The train left HAVRE at 11.55 P.M. The remainder of the Battalion at SOUTHAMPTON sailed for HAVRE at 6 P.M. on S.S. KING EDWARD.

                 POPERINGHE.

31st 12 PM   The 11.55 P.M. from HAVRE reached HAZEBROUCK at 5 P.M.; here, orders were received to proceed to POPERINGHE which place was reached at 8 P.M. After detrainment the Party less Transport were marched with guide to "D" Camp 20th DIVISION; the Transport being led by another

1916   Appendix.

March

31st   guide to their quarters. The
(C'td.)   S.S. KING EDWARD reached HAVRE
             at 6.30 P.M. After disembarking
             the party proceeded to HAVRE
             Rest Camp eventually entraining
             for ROUEN at 11.30 P.M.

APRIL

1st 8 PM.   The Commanding Officer reported
             to 20th D.H.Q. at 9.30 A.M. and
             received instructions as to
             areas of work for Companies.
             The second party reached ROUEN
             at 6 A.M. where it was entrained
             for POPERINGHE at 8.30 P.M.

2nd 8 PM.   At 2 A.M. 2 Officers left Camp
             to report at C.20 nearly
             Central to reconnoitre area of
             work. The second party arrived
             at POPERINGHE at 5.30 P.M. and
             marched to "D" Camp, 20th
             DIVISION. 1 Company left for
             work at C.20 nearly Central at
             6 P.M. but returned owing to
             there being no train arranged
             for, as promised.

             A.30 CENTRAL.

3rd 12 P.M. One Company left at 6 P.M. to
             work on drainage of trenches
             at C.20.d.3.5. Officers left
             during the day to reconnoitre
             areas for work at C.13, about
             Central: and B.12.d.8.6½; B.18
             about Central; and C.22.d.6.4.
             respectively.

             OOSTHOEK   A.30 CENTRAL.

4th 12 A.M. One Company worked on drainage
             of trenches at C.20.d.3.5.

5th 12 A.M. One Company started drainage
             and repairing of parapet at C.13,
             about Central; another Company
             cleared choked up stream at
             C.20.b.3.7., drained a trench at
             C.20.b.3.6. and worked on
             communication trench at C.20.c.3.2½.
             Another Company improved a
             subterranean sap leading to a
             machine gun emplacement, converted
             a shell hole into an observation
             post, made a new cutting 35 feet

1916

Appendix.

April

5th (C'td.) long and made an observation post at B.12.d.8.8. Materials for work for the following night were carried from the dump to B.18. about Central. Approximately 150 yards of tram line were levelled off at B.22.d.6.3. and 250 sleepers were laid and covered from view of enemy aircraft.

6th 12 AM About 250 yards of drainage trench was cleared at C.20.b.3.7. and communication trench at C.20.c.3.2½ was drained by one Company. Another Company were occupied in draining, sandbagging and repairing of parapets of communication trench C.13 about Central. Further materials for work were carried from dump to B.18 about Central, where about 20 yards of wiring were completed by the remaining Company.

7th 12 AM One Company carried out revetting work at C.20.c.3.2½; Trench clearing at C.20.b.3.7. and started a communication Trench at C.20.b.3.7. One man was killed and one slightly wounded. Another Company carried on draining, sandbagging, and repairing of parapet at C.13 about Central. The remaining Company carried on construction of tram line at B.22.d.6.3., ground levelling and sleeper-laying comprised the night's work.

8th 12 AM One Company continued digging trench (communication) at C.20.b.3.7; draining of communication trench at C.20.b.3.7. was also continued and improvements at C.20.c.3.2½ were carried on.
At C.13 about Central, cleaning and revetting of a trench was carried out by one Company, which also employed a number of men in carrying rails, trench boards etc. and wire gabions and U Frames were conveyed to Canal Bridge at C.13.c.2.3. Another Company at B.12.d.8.7. heightened with sandbags a communication trench leading to fire-bay, and improved wall thereof. A new communication trench was changed in

1916   Appendix.

April

8th (C'td) — its alignment and deepened. The same Company cleared obstruction from passage and levelled floor as far as possible, but the subterranean passage could not be continued as pump was out of order.
At B.18, about Central, 40 yards of wiring were completed, while at B.22.d.6.3. nails and sleepers were carried to positions for laying; cutting and levelling for track was also carried out and banking was done as well. The remaining Company continued draining Communication Trench at C.20.b.3.7. A trench at C.20.b.3.7 was revetted, while revetting work was carried on at C.20.c.3.2½.

9th 12 AM — One Company carried out revetting and construction of a parapet and drainage at C.20.c.3.2½, and moved U frames and corrugated iron from C.19.c.5.0. to C.20.b.3.7. where a trench was revetted. Another Company at C.13, about Central, conveyed stores for work from C.13.b.3.2½ to C.13, about Central; drained a communication trench and filled sandbags and made use of same at C.13. about Central. Another Company fixed a pump in sap head at B.12.d.8.7. but unsatisfactory progress was made on account of pump not acting well. The trench in fire bay was deepened and earth was thrown up to thicken parapet. The parapet of a communication trench was built up with sandbags and filled in behind with earth. A trench which had been knocked in by an Aerial Torpedo was partially cleared out, and part of a bombing trench was straightened and deepened. All this took place at B.12.d.8.7. At B.18, about Central, 50 yards of barbed wire entanglements were erected and stakes taken from the Dump. At B.22.d.6.3. about 200 yards of sleepers and rails were laid and banked.

10th 12 AM. — One Company completed repairs to M.G. Sap, revetted 2 Communication trenches by means of sandbags, and finished cutting for Bombing Trench at B.12.b.8.7. While at B.18, about Central, 50 more

1916   Appendix.

April

10th
(C'td.)   yards of wire entanglements were
          erected, pickets were driven in for
          a distance of 50 yards, and a
          start was made for laying two
          new traverses. At B.22.d.6.3. men
          continued with carrying of rails
          and sleepers, and packing along
          tram line. Another Company at
          C.13, about Central, carried on
          repairs and drainage of communica-
          tion trench and continued to
          repair parapets and fill sandbags.
          3 men were wounded. The remaining
          Company carried on improvement of
          parapet at C.20.b.3.7.

11th 12A.M. One Company at B.12.d.8.7. carried
          out sandbag revetting to 2
          communication trenches, worked on
          cutting for bombing straight, and
          pumped M.G. Sap. At B.18, about
          Central, 50 yards of wiring was
          completed, sandbags were filled and
          traverse and fire trench in New X
          line were built. At B.22.d.6.3.
          rails, sleepers and packing for
          tram line were carried up for work.
          Another Company worked on drainage
          and general repair work of
          Communication trench at C.13, about
          Central; one man, a sergeant was
          wounded in the shoulder on leaving
          work. The remaining Company filled
          Sandbags, revetted and built up
          parapet of trench at C.20.c.3.2½
          while at C.20.b.3.7. the new
          communication trench was revetted
          and a further extension of the
          trench was planned and started.
          One man, a lance corporal was
          wounded.

12th 12 AM. Owing to the development of an
          attack on the part of the evening
          between the hours of 6 and 9 P.M.
          only one Company was able to
          proceed with its work. Material
          for work was carried from Dump to
          C.20.c.3.2½ and C.20.b.3.7.

13th 12 AM. One Company worked on tram line
          at B.22.d.6.3. while at B.12.d.8.7.
          hurdles, pickets, wire, mauls, &
          sandbags were carried up to the
          trenches, 8 hurdles being put into
          bombing trench and part of the bomb-
          ing trench being deepened.

1916   Appendix.

April

13th
(C'td.)   At B.18, about Central, candbags were thrown up and the trench was cleared and traverses rebuilt. One man was killed. At B.29.a. a trench 400 yards long was dug and a cable laid in it at a depth of 2 ft. 6 ins. and buried. Another Company revetted and strengthened 100 feet of parapet at C.20.c.3.2½, while 80 yards of new trench was deepened at C.20.b.3.7. where in addition to this work, 30 yards of new trench was dug and communication trench was drained. The remaining Company carried material to trench at C.13, about Central, where digging and repairing the parapet was carried out, and wire revetting and sandbagging was done.

14th 12 AM.   Two drainage trenches were cleared by one Company at C.20, about Crntral, while sandbags were filled and the parapet thickened at trench C.20.c.3.2½. Another Company drained and repaired generally the Communication trench at C.13 about Central. One man was wounded while engaged in filling sandbags. The remaining Company continued sandbag revetting on bombing straight trench at B.12.d.8.7. while wiring and sandbag revetting was carried on at B.18, about Central, 21 men of this party being engaged in carrying material to M.G. emplacement from B.17.d.8.2, and at B.22.d.6.3. packing of tram line was completed and siding for engine house was started.

15th 8 P.M.   Sandbagging and revetting was continued on the Communication Trench by one Company at C.13, about Central; another Company revetted a trench with sandbags, pumped out water, and repaired a bombing straight trench which had been blown up by trench mortars at B.12.d.8.7. while at B.18, about Central, material was carried up from Barrier Dump and wiring was continued. Carrying for M.G. Emplacement was carried out from B.17.d.8.2.; the same Company also

1916   Appendix.

April

15th
(C'td.)   supplied labour on engine shed
             branch line at B.22.d.6.3.
             packing of tramway beyond junction
             was done, rails were carried &
             trollies with rails and material
             were shunted.
             Carrying and packing generally
             was continued from Canal side of
             tramway. The remaining Company
             worked on Trench parapet at
             C.20.c.3.2½ and continued working
             at C.20, about Central.
             The Battalion marched out from
             A.30, central, at 10.35 A.M.,
             arriving with Field Kitchens at
             "J" Camp about 4 p.m.

             "J" CAMP, POPERINGHE.

16th 8 pm.   The Battalion and all transport
             arrived about 4.30 p.m. at
             "J", 17.a. and was in billets
             by 6 P.M.

             "J" 17.a. WINNEZEELE.

17th 8 pm.   The Battalion commenced training
             according to scheme of work
             submitted to D.H.Q. - (Platoon
             and squad drill and musketry)
             the latter being rendered
             difficult owing to the entire
             absence of musketry instruction
             appliances, and to the battalion
             possessing only 230 rifles.
             These were obtained on instructions
             from D.H.Q. Unfortunately this
             total was all that could be spared,
             which fact strongly emphasises
             the need for a plentiful supply of
             arms to be available for divisional
             and other troops. The somewhat
             exceptional circumstances under
             which the unit arrived at a danger
             zone to work, should have influenced
             the home authorities to see that
             rifles were provided for the
             Battalion on its arrival at such
             a destination.

18th 8 pm.   Training in squad and platoon drill
             and musketry continued.

19th 8 pm.   Training in squad drill, extended
             order drill & musketry.

1916

Appendix.

April

20th 8 PM. The usual instruction carried out.

21st 8 PM Training was carried on during morning only.

22nd 8 PM Morning programme carried out.

23rd 8 PM Sunday observed as a day of rest.

24th 8 PM. Pioneer training commenced in conjunction with R.E. Field Company. Two Companies employed on digging and revetting fire trench and traffic trench. Remaining two Companies continued training in Musketry, less one Platoon told off to erect barbed wire entanglements.

25th 8 PM Pioneering and Musketry as on previous day.

26th 8 PM Sandbagging, revetting and wiring practice; musketry instruction. One N.C.O. and ten men detailed to erect range of 30 yards in disused farmhouse.

27th 8 PM. Trench digging and musketry training. One Officer and 50 men detailed to cut brush wood for making of fascines.

28th 8 PM. 30 yards range completed with exception of targets. Musketry and trench digging and wiring was carried out as per training scheme. Fascine making was commenced.

29th 8 PM. The Battalion marched by Companies to C.16.b. to get washed and to receive change of underclothing.

30th 8 PM. The four Companies received 500 dummy cartridges each, they also were issued with two aiming tripods apiece. During the past week, improvised aiming discs and targets were employed in the training of men.
*The battalion will commence on the first of next month the firing course (Table A) on the 30 yard range, sufficient white paper having been purchased for the purpose of making a stock of targets.

*Observation by C.O. on progress of two weeks training.

1916   Appendix.

April

30th (C'td.)   The training received during the first two weeks of the resting period has been satisfactory in spite of rather primitive arrangements for musketry. The intelligent interest evinced by the men and the instruction imparted by Officers contributed largely to the rate of progress. The helpful suggestion and supervision of the R.E. Officers produced good work in trench digging, revetting, wiring and general pioneer work.

20th BATTALION. THE KING'S ROYAL RIFLE CORPS.

1916   Appendix.

March   SOUTHAMPTON.

27th 11 PM.   The 20th (S) Battalion, K.R.R.C.
              (B.E.L. Pioneers) left Wellingboro'
              in three trains at 7.15 a.m., 9.0 am,
              and 10.20 a.m. respectively, arriv-
              ing at SOUTHAMPTON at 2.30 p.m.,
              4 p.m. and 5 p.m. The Battalion
              embarked on two (2) ships; 10 Officers
              212 other ranks and Transport on the
              ROSSETTI, and 18 Officers, 772 other
              ranks on the MARGUERETTE.
              The MARGUERETTE sailed; the ROSSETTI
              attempted the voyage, but received
              orders to return and anchor in the
              SOLENT owing to bad weather.

28th 11 PM   The ROSSETTI remained at anchor till
              4.30 P.M., meanwhile the MARGUERETTE
              returned to SOUTHAMPTON at 12 noon
              having suffered considerably from
              heavy seas. The 18 Officers and 772
              other ranks proceeded to the Rest
              Camp at SOUTHAMPTON for the night.
              The ROSSETTI made another attempt
              to sail, but returned once more to
              the SOLENT and anchored for the night.

29th 11 PM   The ROSSETTI left for HAVRE at
              4.30 P.M. The remainder of the
              Battalion remained at the SOUTHAMPTON
              Rest Camp.

HAVRE.

30th 12 PM   The ROSSETTI reached HAVRE at 4 a.m.
              At 7 A.M. all ranks and Transport
              were disembarked, with orders to
              remain at HAVRE dock until 8 P.M.
              when party marched to entrain at GARE
              DE MARCHANDISE. The train left HAVRE
              at 11.55 P.M. The remainder of the
              Battalion at SOUTHAMPTON sailed for
              HAVRE at 6 P.M. on S.S. KING EDWARD.

POPERINGHE.

31st 12 PM   The 11.55 P.M. from HAVRE reached
              HAZEBROUCK at 5 P.M.; here, orders
              were received to proceed to
              POPERINGHE which place was reached
              at 8 P.M. After detrainment the
              Party less Transport were marched
              with guide to "D" Camp 20th DIVISION;
              the Transport being led by another

1916   Appendix.

March

31st   guide to their quarters. The
(C'td.)   S.S. KING EDWARD reached HAVRE
            at 6.30 P.M. After disembarking
            the party proceeded to HAVRE
            Rest Camp eventually entraining
            for ROUEN at 11.30 P.M.

APRIL

1st 8 PM.   The Commanding Officer reported
            to 20th D.H.Q. at 9.30 A.M. and
            received instructions as to
            areas of work for Companies.
            The second party reached ROUEN
            at 6 A.M. where it was entrained
            for POPERINGHE at 8.30 P.M.

2nd 8 PM.   At 2 A.M. 2 Officers left Camp
            to report at C.20 nearly
            Central to reconnoitre area of
            work. The second party arrived
            at POPERINGHE at 5.30 P.M. and
            marched to "D" Camp, 20th
            DIVISION. 1 Company left for
            work at C.20 nearly Central at
            6 P.M. but returned owing to
            there being no train arranged
            for, as promised.

            A.30 CENTRAL.

3rd 12 P.M. One Company left at 6 P.M. to
            work on drainage of trenches
            at C.20.d.3.5. Officers left
            during the day to reconnoitre
            areas for work at C.13, about
            Central: and B.12.d.8.6½; B.18
            about Central; and C.22.d.6.4.
            respectively.

            OOSTHOEK A.30 CENTRAL.

4th 12 A.M. One Company worked on drainage
            of trenches at C.20.d.3.5.

5th 12 A.M. One Company started drainage
            and repairing of parapet at C.13,
            about Central; another Company
            cleared choked up stream at
            C.20.b.3.7., drained a trench at
            C.20.b.3.6. and worked on
            communication trench at C.20.c.3.2½.
            Another Company improved a
            subterranean sap leading to a
            machine gun emplacement, converted
            a shell hole into an observation
            post, made a new cutting 35 feet

1916   Appendix.

April

5th
(C'td.)   long and made an observation post at B.12.d.8.8. Materials for work for the following night were carried from the dump to B.18. about Central. Approximately 150 yards of tram line were levelled off at B.22.d.6.3. and 250 sleepers were laid and covered from view of enemy aircraft.

6th 12 AM   About 250 yards of drainage trench was cleared at C.20.b.3.7. and communication trench at C.20.c.3.2½ was drained by one Company. Another Company were occupied in draining, sandbagging and repairing of parapets of communication trench C.13 about Central. Further materials for work were carried from dump to B.18 about Central, where about 20 yards of wiring were completed by the remaining Company.

7th 12 AM   One Company carried out revetting work at C.20.c.3.2½; Trench clearing at C.20.b.3.7. and started a communication Trench at C.20.b.3.7. One man was killed and one slightly wounded. Another Company carried on draining, sandbagging, and repairing of parapet at C.13 about Central. The remaining Company carried on construction of tram line at B.22.d.6.3., ground levelling and sleeper-laying comprised the night's work.

8th 12 AM   One Company continued digging trench (communication) at C.20.b.3.7; draining of communication trench at C.20.b.3.7. was also continued and improvements at C.20.c.3.2½ were carried on.
At C.13 about Central, cleaning and revetting of a trench was carried out by one Company, which also employed a number of men in carrying rails, trench boards etc. and wire gabions and U Frames were conveyed to Canal Bridge at C.13.c.2.3. Another Company at B.12.d.8.7. heightened with sandbags a communication trench leading to fire-bay, and improved wall thereof. A new communication trench was changed in

1916   Appendix.

April

8th   its alignment and deepened. The
(C'td)   same Company cleared obstruction
             from passage and levelled floor
             as far as possible, but the
             subterranean passage could not be
             continued as pump was out of
             order.
             At B.18, about Central, 40 yards
             of wiring were completed, while
             at B.22.d.6.3. nails and sleepers
             were carried to positions for
             laying; cutting and levelling for
             track was also carried out and
             banking was done as well. The
             remaining Company continued drain-
             ing Communication Trench at
             C.20.b.3.7. A trench at C.20.b.3.7.
             was revetted, while revetting work
             was carried on at C.20.c.3.2½.

9th 12 AM   One Company carried out revetting
             and construction of a parapet and
             drainage at C.20.c.3.2½, and moved
             U frames and corrugated iron from
             C.19.c.5.0. to C.20.b.3.7. where a
             trench was revetted. Another
             Company at C.13, about Central,
             conveyed stores for work from
             C.13.b.3.2½ to C.13, about Central;
             drained a communication trench and
             filled sandbags and made use of
             same at C.13. about Central.
             Another Company fixed a pump in sap
             head at B.12.d.8.7. but unsatisfactory
             progress was made on account of pump
             not acting well. The trench in fire
             bay was deepened and earth was thrown
             up to thicken parapet. The parapet
             of a communication trench was built
             up with sandbags and filled in behind
             with earth. A trench which had been
             knocked in by an Aerial Torpedo was
             partially cleared out, and part of
             a bombing trench was straightened
             and deepened. All this took place
             at B.12.d.8.7. At B.18, about Central,
             50 yards of barbed wire entanglements
             were erected and stakes taken from the
             Dump. At B.22.d.6.3. about 200 yards
             of sleepers and rails were laid and
             banked.

10th 12 AM. One Company completed repairs to M.G.
             Sap, revetted 2 Communication trenches
             by means of sandbags, and finished
             cutting for Bombing Trench at B.12.b.8.7.
             While at B.18, about Central, 50 more

1916   Appendix.

April

10th
(C'td.)   yards of wire entanglements were
            erected, pickets were driven in for
            a distance of 50 yards, and a
            start was made for laying two
            new traverses. At B.22.d.6.3. men
            continued with carrying of rails
            and sleepers, and packing along
            tram line. Another Company at
            C.13, about Central, carried on
            repairs and drainage of communica-
            tion trench and continued to
            repair parapets and fill sandbags.
            3 men were wounded. The remaining
            Company carried on improvement of
            parapet at C.20.b.3.7.

11th 12A.M. One Company at B.12.d.8.7. carried
            out sandbag revetting to 2
            communication trenches, worked on
            cutting for bombing straight, and
            pumped M.G. Sap. At B.18, about
            Central, 50 yards of wiring was
            completed, sandbags were filled and
            traverse and fire trench in New X
            line were built. At B.22.d.6.3.
            rails, sleepers and packing for
            tram line were carried up for work.
            Another Company worked on drainage
            and general repair work of
            Communication trench at C.13, about
            Central; one man, a sergeant was
            wounded in the shoulder on leaving
            work. The remaining Company filled
            Sandbags, revetted and built up
            parapet of trench at C.20.c.3.2½
            while at C.20.b.3.7. the new
            communication trench was revetted
            and a further extension of the
            trench was planned and started.
            One man, a lance corporal was
            wounded.

12th 12 AM. Owing to the development of an
            attack on the part of the evening
            between the hours of 6 and 9 P.M.
            only one Company was able to
            proceed with its work. Material
            for work was carried from Dump to
            C.20.c.3.2½ and C.20.b.3.7.

13th 12 AM. One Company worked on tram line
            at B.22.d.6.3. while at B.12.d.8.7.
            hurdles, pickets, wire, mauls, &
            sandbags were carried up to the
            trenches, 8 hurdles being put into
            bombing trench and part of the bomb-
            ing trench being deepened.

1916   Appendix.

April

13th   At B.18, about Central, sandbags
(C'td.)   were thrown up and the trench was
            cleared and traverses rebuilt.
            One man was killed. At B.29.a.
            a trench 400 yards long was dug
            and a cable laid in it at a depth
            of 2 ft. 6 ins. and buried.
            Another Company revetted and
            strengthened 100 feet of parapet
            at C.20.c.3.2½, while 80 yards of
            new trench was deepened at
            C.20.b.3.7. where in addition to
            this work, 30 yards of new trench
            was dug and communication trench
            was drained. The remaining
            Company carried material to trench
            at C.13, about Central, where
            digging and repairing the parapet
            was carried out, and wire revetting
            and sandbagging was done.

14th 12 AM. Two drainage trenches were cleared
            by one Company at C.20, about
            Crntral, while sandbags were filled
            and the parapet thickened at trench
            C.20.c.3.2½. Another Company
            drained and repaired generally the
            Communication trench at C.13 about
            Central. One man was wounded
            while engaged in filling sandbags.
            The remaining Company continued
            sandbag revetting on bombing
            straight trench at B.12.d.8.7.
            while wiring and sandbag revetting
            was carried on at B.18, about
            Central, 21 men of this party
            being engaged in carrying material
            to M.G. emplacement from B.17.d.8.2,
            and at B.22.d.6.3. packing of tram
            line was completed and siding for
            engine house was started.

15th 8 P.M. Sandbagging and revetting was
            continued on the Communication
            Trench by one Company at C.13,
            about Central; another Company
            revetted a trench with sandbags,
            pumped out water, and repaired a
            bombing straight trench which
            had been blown up by trench mortars
            at B.12.d.8.7. while at B.18, about
            Central, material was carried up
            from Barrier Dump and wiring was
            continued. Carrying for M.G.
            Emplacement was carried out from
            B.17.d.8.2.; the same Company also

1916   Appendix.

April

15th   supplied labour on engine shed
(C'td.)   branch line at B.22.d.6.3.
             packing of tramway beyond junction
             was done, rails were carried &
             trollies with rails and material
             were shunted.
             Carrying and packing generally
             was continued from Canal side of
             tramway. The remaining Company
             worked on Trench parapet at
             C.20.c.3.2½ and continued working
             at C.20, about Central.
             The Battalion marched out from
             A.30, central, at 10.35 A.M.,
             arriving with Field Kitchens at
             "J" Camp about 4 p.m.

             "J" CAMP, POPERINGHE.

16th 8 pm.   The Battalion and all transport
             arrived about 4.30 p.m. at
             "J", 17.a. and was in billets
             by 6 P.M.

             "J" 17.a. WINNEZEELE.

17th 8 pm.   The Battalion commenced training
             according to scheme of work
             submitted to D.H.Q. - (Platoon
             and squad drill and musketry)
             the latter being rendered
             difficult owing to the entire
             absence of musketry instruction
             appliances, and to the battalion
             possessing only 230 rifles.
             These were obtained on instructions
             from D.H.Q. Unfortunately this
             total was all that could be spared,
             which fact strongly emphasises
             the need for a plentiful supply of
             arms to be available for divisional
             and other troops. The somewhat
             exceptional circumstances under
             which the unit arrived at a danger
             zone to work should have influenced
             the home authorities to see that
             rifles were provided for the
             Battalion on its arrival at such
             a destination.

18th 8 pm.   Training in squad and platoon drill
             and musketry continued.

19th 8 pm.   Training in squad drill, extended
             order drill & musketry.

1916   Appendix.

April

20th 8 PM.   The usual instruction carried out.

21st 8 PM   Training was carried on during
             morning only.

22nd 8 PM   Morning programme carried out.

23rd 8 PM   Sunday observed as a day of rest.

24th 8 PM.   Pioneer training commenced in
             conjunction with R.E. Field
             Company. Two Companies employed
             on digging and revetting fire
             trench and traffic trench.
             Remaining two Companies continued
             training in Musketry, less one
             Platoon told off to erect barbed
             wire entanglements.

25th 8 PM   Pioneering and Musketry as on
             previous day.

26th 8 PM   Sandbagging, revetting and wiring
             practice; musketry instruction.
             One N.C.O. and ten men detailed
             to erect range of 30 yards in
             disused farmhouse.

27th 8 PM.   Trench digging and musketry
             training. One Officer and 50
             men detailed to cut brush wood
             for making of fascines.

28th 8 PM.   30 yards range completed with
             exception of targets. Musketry
             and trench digging and wiring
             was carried out as per training
             scheme. Fascine making was
             commenced.

29th 8 PM.   The Battalion marched by Companies
             to C.16.b. to get washed and to
             receive change of underclothing.

30th 8 PM.   The four Companies received 500
             dummy cartridges each, they also
             were issued with two aiming
             tripods apiece. During the past
             week, improvised aiming discs
             and targets were employed in the
             training of men.
             *The battalion will commence on the
             first of next month the firing
             course (Table A) on the 30 yard
             range, sufficient white paper having
             been purchased for the purpose of
             making a stock of targets.

             *Observation by C.O. on progress of
             two weeks training.

1916   Appendix.

April

30th   The training received during
(C'td.)   the first two weeks of the rest-
            ing period has been satisfactory
            in spite of rather primitive
            arrangements for musketry.
            The intelligent interest evinced
            by the men and the instruction
            imparted by Officers contributed
            largely to the rate of progress.
            The helpful suggestion and
            supervision of the R.E. Officers
            produced good work in trench
            digging, revetting, wiring and
            general pioneer work.

20th BATTALION, THE KING'S ROYAL RIFLE CORPS.

1916 Appendix.

March SOUTHAMPTON.

27th 11 PM. The 20th (S) Battalion, K.R.R.C. (B.E.F. Pioneers) left Wellingboro' in three trains at 7.15 a.m., 9.0 am, and 10.20 a.m. respectively, arriving at SOUTHAMPTON at 2.30 p.m., 4 p.m. and 5 p.m. The Battalion embarked on two (2) ships; 10 Officers 212 other ranks and Transport on the ROSSETTI, and 18 Officers, 772 other ranks on the MARGUERETTE. The MARGUERETTE sailed; the ROSSETTI attempted the voyage, but received orders to return and anchor in the SOLENT owing to bad weather.

28th 11 PM The ROSSETTI remained at anchor till 4.30 P.M., meanwhile the MARGUERETTE returned to SOUTHAMPTON at 12 noon having suffered considerably from heavy seas. The 18 Officers and 772 other ranks proceeded to the Rest Camp at SOUTHAMPTON for the night. The ROSSETTI made another attempt to sail, but returned once more to the SOLENT and anchored for the night.

29th 11 PM The ROSSETTI left for HAVRE at 4.30 P.M. The remainder of the Battalion remained at the SOUTHAMPTON Rest Camp.

HAVRE.

30th 12 PM The ROSSETTI reached HAVRE at 4 a.m. At 7 A.M. all ranks and Transport were disembarked, with orders to remain at HAVRE dock until 8 P.M. when party marched to entrain at GARE DE MARCHANDISE. The train left HAVRE at 11.55 P.M. The remainder of the Battalion at SOUTHAMPTON sailed for HAVRE at 6 P.M. on S.S. KING EDWARD.

POPERINGHE.

31st 12 PM The 11.55 P.M. from HAVRE reached HAZEBROUCK at 5 P.M.; here, orders were received to proceed to POPERINGHE which place was reached at 8 P.M. After detrainment the Party less Transport were marched with guide to "D" Camp 20th DIVISION; the Transport being led by another

1916   Appendix.

March

31st
(C'td.)   guide to their quarters. The
          S.S. KING EDWARD reached HAVRE
          at 6.30 P.M. After disembarking
          the party proceeded to HAVRE
          Rest Camp eventually entraining
          for ROUEN at 11.30 P.M.

APRIL

1st 8 PM. The Commanding Officer reported
           to 20th D.H.Q. at 9.30 A.M. and
           received instructions as to
           areas of work for Companies.
           The second party reached ROUEN
           at 6 A.M. where it was entrained
           for POPERINGHE at 8.30 P.M.

2nd 8 PM. At 2 A.M. 2 Officers left Camp
           to report at C.20 nearly
           Central to reconnoitre area of
           work. The second party arrived
           at POPERINGHE at 5.30 P.M. and
           marched to "D" Camp, 20th
           DIVISION. 1 Company left for
           work at C.20 nearly Central at
           6 P.M. but returned owing to
           there being no train arranged
           for, as promised.

           A.30 CENTRAL.

3rd 12 P.M. One Company left at 6 P.M. to
            work on drainage of trenches
            at C.20.d.3.5. Officers left
            during the day to reconnoitre
            areas for work at C.13, about
            Central: and B.12.d.8.6½; B.18
            about Central; and C.22.d.6.4.
            respectively.

            OOSTHOEK A.30 CENTRAL.

4th 12 A.M. One Company worked on drainage
            of trenches at C.20.d.3.5.

5th 12 A.M. One Company started drainage
            and repairing of parapet at C.13,
            about Central; another Company
            cleared choked up stream at
            C.20.b.3.7., drained a trench at
            C.20.b.3.6. and worked on
            communication trench at C.20.c.3.2½.
            Another Company improved a
            subterranean sap leading to a
            machine gun emplacement, converted
            a shell hole into an observation
            post, made a new cutting 35 feet

1916   Appendix.

April

5th (C'td.) long and made an observation post at B.12.d.8.8. Materials for work for the following night were carried from the dump to B.18. about Central. Approximately 150 yards of tram line were levelled off at B.22.d.6.3. and 250 sleepers were laid and covered from view of enemy aircraft.

6th 12 AM About 250 yards of drainage trench was cleared at C.20.b.3.7. and communication trench at C.20.c.3.2½ was drained by one Company. Another Company were occupied in draining, sandbagging and repairing of parapets of communication trench C.13 about Central. Further materials for work were carried from dump to B.18 about Central, where about 20 yards of wiring were completed by the remaining Company.

7th 12 AM One Company carried out revetting work at C.20.c.3.2½; Trench clearing at C.20.b.3.7. and started a communication trench at C.20.b.3.7. One man was killed and one slightly wounded. Another Company carried on draining, sandbagging, and repairing of parapet at C.13 about Central. The remaining Company carried on construction of tram line at B.22.d.6.3., ground levelling and sleeper-laying comprised the night's work.

8th 12 AM One Company continued digging trench (communication) at C.20.b.3.7; draining of communication trench at C.20.b.3.7. was also continued and improvements at C.20.c.3.2½ were carried on.
At C.13 about Central, cleaning and revetting of a trench was carried out by one Company, which also employed a number of men in carrying rails, trench boards etc. and wire gabions and U Frames were conveyed to Canal Bridge at C.13.c.2.3. Another Company at B.12.d.8.7. heightened with sandbags a communication trench leading to fire-bay, and improved wall thereof. A new communication trench was changed in

1916   Appendix.

April

8th   its alignment and deepened. The
(C'td)   same Company cleared obstruction
           from passage and levelled floor
           as far as possible, but the
           subterranean passage could not be
           continued as pump was out of
           order.
           At B.18, about Central, 40 yards
           of wiring were completed, while
           at B.22.d.6.3. nails and sleepers
           were carried to positions for
           laying; cutting and levelling for
           track was also carried out and
           banking was done as well. The
           remaining Company continued drain-
           ing Communication Trench at
           C.20.b.3.7. A trench at C.20.b.3.7
           was revetted, while revetting work
           was carried on at C.20.c.3.2½.

9th 12 AM One Company carried out revetting
           and construction of a parapet and
           drainage at C.20.c.3.2½, and moved
           U frames and corrugated iron from
           C.19.c.5.0. to C.20.b.3.7. where a
           trench was revetted. Another
           Company at C.13, about Central,
           conveyed stores for work from
           C.13.b.3.2½ to C.13, about Central;
           drained a communication trench and
           filled sandbags and made use of
           same at C.13, about Central.
           Another Company fixed a pump in sap
           head at B.12.d.8.7. but unsatisfactory
           progress was made on account of pump
           not acting well. The trench in fire
           bay was deepened and earth was thrown
           up to thicken parapet. The parapet
           of a communication trench was built
           up with sandbags and filled in behind
           with earth. A trench which had been
           knocked in by an Aerial Torpedo was
           partially cleared out, and part of
           a bombing trench was straightened
           and deepened. All this took place
           at B.12.d.8.7. At B.18, about Central,
           50 yards of barbed wire entanglements
           were erected and stakes taken from the
           Dump. At B.22.d.6.3. about 200 yards
           of sleepers and rails were laid and
           banked.

10th 12 AM. One Company completed repairs to M.G.
           Sap, revetted 2 Communication trenches
           by means of sandbags, and finished
           cutting for Bombing Trench at B.12.b.8.7.
           While at B.18, about Central, 50 more

1916   Appendix.

April

10th
(C'td.)   yards of wire entanglements were
          erected, pickets were driven in for
          a distance of 50 yards, and a
          start was made for laying two
          new traverses. At B.22.d.6.3. men
          continued with carrying of rails
          and sleepers, and packing along
          tram line. Another Company at
          C.13, about Central, carried on
          repairs and drainage of communica-
          tion trench and continued to
          repair parapets and fill sandbags.
          3 men were wounded. The remaining
          Company carried on improvement of
          parapet at C.20.b.3.7.

11th 12A.M. One Company at B.12.d.8.7. carried
          out sandbag revetting to 2
          communication trenches, worked on
          cutting for bombing straight, and
          pumped M.G. Sap. At B.18, about
          Central, 50 yards of wiring was
          completed, sandbags were filled and
          traverse and fire trench in New X
          line were built. At B.22.d.6.3.
          rails, sleepers and packing for
          tram line were carried up for work.
          Another Company worked on drainage
          and general repair work of
          Communication trench at C.13, about
          Central; one man, a Sergeant was
          wounded in the shoulder on leaving
          work. The remaining Company filled
          Sandbags, revetted and built up
          parapet of trench at C.20.c.3.2½
          while at C.20.b.3.7. the new
          communication trench was revetted
          and a further extension of the
          trench was planned and started.
          One man, a lance corporal was
          wounded.

12th 12 AM. Owing to the development of an
          attack on the part of the evening
          between the hours of 6 and 9 P.M.
          only one Company was able to
          proceed with its work. Material
          for work was carried from Dump to
          C.20.c.3.2½ and C.20.b.3.7.

13th 12 AM. One Company worked on tram line
          at B.22.d.6.3. while at B.12.d.8.7.
          hurdles, pickets, wire, mauls, &
          sandbags were carried up to the
          trenches, 6 hurdles being put into
          bombing trench and part of the bomb-
          ing trench being deepened.

1916   Appendix.

April

13th (C'td.) At B.18, about Central, sandbags were thrown up and the trench was cleared and traverses rebuilt. One man was killed. At B.29.a. a trench 400 yards long was dug and a cable laid in it at a depth of 2 ft. 6 ins. and buried. Another Company revetted and strengthened 100 feet of parapet at C.20.c.3.2½, while 80 yards of new trench was deepened at C.20.b.3.7, where in addition to this work, 30 yards of new trench was dug and communication trench was drained. The remaining Company carried material to trench at C.13, about Central, where digging and repairing the parapet was carried out, and wire revetting and sandbagging was done.

14th 12 AM. Two drainage trenches were cleared by one Company at C.20, about Central, while sandbags were filled and the parapet thickened at trench C.20.c.3.2½. Another Company drained and repaired generally the Communication trench at C.13 about Central. One man was wounded while engaged in filling sandbags. The remaining Company continued sandbag revetting on bombing straight trench at B.12.d.8.7. while wiring and sandbag revetting was carried on at B.18, about Central, 21 men of this party being engaged in carrying material to M.G. emplacement from B.17.d.6.2, and at B.22.d.6.3. packing of tram line was completed and siding for engine house was started.

15th 8 P.M. Sandbagging and revetting was continued on the Communication Trench by one Company at C.13, about Central; another Company revetted a trench with sandbags, pumped out water, and repaired a bombing straight trench which had been blown up by trench mortars at B.12.d.8.7. while at B.18, about Central, material was carried up from Barrier Dump and wiring was continued. Carrying for M.G. Emplacement was carried out from B.17.d.8.2.; the same Company also

1916   Appendix.

April

15th   supplied labour on engine shed
(C'td.)   branch line at B.22.d.6.3.
              packing of tramway beyond junction
              was done, rails were carried &
              trollies with rails and material
              were shunted.
              Carrying and packing generally
              was continued from Canal side of
              tramway. The remaining Company
              worked on French parapet at
              C.20.c.3.2½ and continued working
              at C.30, about Central.
              The Battalion marched out from
              A.30, central, at 10.30 A.M.,
              arriving with Field Kitchens at
              "J" Camp about 4 p.m.

              "J" CAMP. POPERINGHE.

16th 8 pm.   The Battalion and all transport
              arrived about 4.30 p.m. at
              "J", 17.a. and was in billets
              by 6 P.M.

              "J" 17.a. WINNEZEELE.

17th 8 pm.   The Battalion commenced training
              according to scheme of work
              submitted to D.H.Q. - (Platoon
              and squad drill and musketry)
              the latter being rendered
              difficult owing to the entire
              absence of musketry instruction
              appliances, and to the battalion
              possessing only 230 rifles.
              These were obtained on instructions
              from D.H.Q. Unfortunately this
              total was all that could be spared,
              which fact strongly emphasises
              the need for a plentiful supply of
              arms to be available for divisional
              and other troops. The somewhat
              exceptional circumstances under
              which the unit arrived at a danger
              zone to work, should have influenced
              the home authorities to see that
              rifles were provided for the
              Battalion on its arrival at such
              a destination.

18th 8 pm.   Training in squad and platoon drill
              and musketry continued.

19th 8 pm.   Training in squad drill, extended
              order drill & musketry.

1916   Appendix.

April

20th 8 PM.   The usual instruction carried out.

21st 8 PM   Training was carried on during
             morning only.

22nd 8 PM   Morning programme carried out.

23rd 8 PM   Sunday observed as a day of rest.

24th 8 PM.   Pioneer training commenced in
             conjunction with R.E. Field
             Company. Two Companies employed
             on digging and revetting fire
             trench and traffic trench.
             Remaining two Companies continued
             training in Musketry, less one
             Platoon told off to erect barbed
             wire entanglements.

25th 8 PM   Pioneering and Musketry as on
             previous day.

26th 8 PM   Sandbagging, revetting and wiring
             practice; musketry instruction.
             One N.C.O. and ten men detailed
             to erect range of 30 yards in
             disused farmhouse.

27th 8 PM.   Trench digging and musketry
             training. One Officer and 50
             men detailed to cut brush wood
             for making of fascines.

28th 8 PM.   30 yards range completed with
             exception of targets. Musketry
             and trench digging and wiring
             was carried out as per training
             scheme. Fascine making was
             commenced.

29th 8 PM.   The Battalion marched by Companies
             to C.16.b. to get washed and to
             receive change of underclothing.

30th 8 PM.   The four Companies received 500
             dummy cartridges each, they also
             were issued with two aiming
             tripods apiece. During the past
             week, improvised aiming discs
             and targets were employed in the
             training of men.
             *The battalion will commence on the
             first of next month the firing
             course (Table A) on the 30 yard
             range, sufficient white paper having
             been purchased for the purpose of
             making a stock of targets.

             *Observation by C.O. on progress of
             two weeks training.

1916   Appendix.

April

30th (C'td.)   The training received during the first two weeks of the resting period has been satisfactory in spite of rather primitive arrangements for musketry. The intelligent interest evinced by the men and the instruction imparted by Officers contributed largely to the rate of progress. The helpful suggestion and supervision of the R.E. Officers produced good work in trench digging, revetting, wiring and general pioneer work.

20. KRRC
Vol 9

Confidential.

War Diary
of 2 Bt. III Bde June
20th Bn. KINGS ROYAL RIFLE CORPS.

from 1st May 1916 to 31st May 1916.
(Volume 2.)

WAR DIARY
or
INTELLIGENCE SUMMARY

(Erase heading not required.)

Army Form C. 2118.

Place	Date	Hour	Summary of Events and Information	Remarks and references to Appendices
J.17.a.	1/5/16	12 P.M.	Training carried out in engineering work night and day and in musketry.	
J.17.a	2/5/16	12 P.M.	Training continued in engineering work night and day and musketry	
J.17.a	3/5/16	12 P.M.	Training continued in engineering work night and day and musketry	
J.17.a	4/5/16	12 P.M.	Training continued in engineering work night and day and musketry	
J.17.a	5/5/16	12 P.M.	Training continued in engineering work night and day and musketry	
J.17.a	6/5/16	4 P.M.	Training continued in musketry and engineering until 12 noon. Day proved a holiday.	
J.17.a	7/5/16	8 P.M.	Training continued in engineering work and musketry.	
J.17.a	8/5/16	12 P.M.	The Battalion less 2 Companies marched out to J.17.a at 9.30 a.m. and arrived in camp at A.9.B.5.2. at 11.30 P.M. The 2 Companies left behind at J.17.a were conveyed after 2 P.M. by motor lorries to H.5. Central, where they were safely billeted for the night.	
A.9.B.8.2.	10/5/16	12 P.M.	General training carried on at A.9.B.8.2:- At H.5 central 2 officers reported by day to O.C. 125 Field Company R.E. to receive orders for work.	

WAR DIARY
or
INTELLIGENCE SUMMARY
(Erase heading not required.)

Army Form C. 2118.

Place	Date	Hour	Summary of Events and Information	Remarks and references to Appendices
A,9,B,8,2	11/5/16	12 PM	General training carried on at A,9,B,8,2;— The two companies at H,5, Central supplied working parties to go to C,13, about Central and C,13, 6, 7, 2; but work was cancelled for that night on account of casualties. Four casualties occurred during the day in 4 ranks of camp & Ball 22.	
A,9,6,8,2	12/5/16	12 PM	General training carried on at A,9,4,8,2;— From H,5, 6ts 6. the found work party was received; at B,29, Central, work continued on 3rd water Tank, while three new water tanks were erected at B,22, Central. At C,13, about central another party completed digging required depth of new trench and party finished deviation slightly packing of sandbags and continued revetment & clearance for draining. 2 Rull trench. Upper portion of rev. trench was retained. The other company started on new communication trench at C,13, C,1,7,2, revetted drove in stakes and cut down sides of trench. Far head of the trench was cleaned up and widened.	
A,9,4,8,2	13/5/16	12 PM	General training carried on at A,9,B,8,2 during the morning. One company at C,13, about Central, carried footboards for new communication trench to that sandbags and sandbagged old com. trench owing to the state of new trench, the whole party had to be put on the (new trench for sandbagging). JB	

WAR DIARY
or
INTELLIGENCE SUMMARY

Army Form C. 2118.

Place	Date	Hour	Summary of Events and Information	Remarks and references to Appendices
A.9, 6, 8, 2	13/5/16	12 P.M.	The other Company deepened the whole length of trench at C,13, 9, 8, 2 down to 3'6" and cleared track the earth about 30" from the edge of the trench. Sandbags were also filled and laid on the edge of the trench; the new work was concealed on the left. Revetting was carried out. The new hurdles were also carried on, and the hurdles were cleaned giving back hurdles having taken place owing to the rain. A drainage out (several slits being 7 ft wide and 3 ft deep was dug, and another Trench 30 yards long 7 ft wide and 3 ft 6" deep. Made 18 yards long 7 ft wide and 3 ft 6" deep.	
A.9, 6, 8, 2	14/5/16	12 P.M.	No training at A,9,6,8,2. One Company at C,13, about cutting Sandbagged Parapets for old communication trench, and then carried out drainage. Sandbagging and repair work to new communication trench. The other Company revetted with sandbags the trench at C,13, c,9,2, one man being wounded. Hurdles were carried from railway dump to site of work, where more men carried out hurdling and wiring. Two main drainage trenches were also completed in this area. General training carried on at – A,9, 6, 8, 2.	
A,9, 6, 8, 2	15/5/16	12 P.M.	C,13, about central filled sandbags and repaired old trench. Drainage filled and new trench was also carried out. Sandbags were filled by another party which continued building parapet and repairing trench. A fatigue from Coy. commn'ds between "W6" bridge and new communication trench. Revetting material was carried up to new old trench also.	

2449 Wt. W14957/Mgo 750,000 1/16 J.B.C. & A. Forms/C.2118/12.

WAR DIARY
or
INTELLIGENCE SUMMARY

Army Form C. 2118.

Place	Date	Hour	Summary of Events and Information	Remarks and references to Appendices
A.9,6,8,2	15/5/16	12 P.M.	Another Company at C,13,C,9,2, carried hurdles and pickets to trench when revetting and wiring was done. Sandbags were also conveyed to S.I.G. & work were sandbagging of new trench was continued.	
A.9,6,8,2	16/5/16	12 P.M.	General training carried on at A,9,6,8,2. One Company at C,13, about central continues repairing & & communication trench, building parapet, training and revetting new communication trench. The barrier was built connective communication trench with W6 hurdles and general material were carried up for work at C,13,C,9,12, continued communication trench. Another Company at C,13,C,9,12, carried french sand continued carrying hurdles and pickets for revetting french, and continued sand bagging french boards were carried up to communication trench. General training carried on at A,9,6,8,2. One Company at	
A,9,6,8,2	17/5/16	12 P.M.	C,13, about central, continued on erection of barrier to connect new C.T. with 6.W. bridge. Footboards were fixed out, hurdles put up, and trench drained. Old trench was hurdled with hurdles and sandbags. Another Company at C,13,C,9,12, carried french boards and sandbags from dump to trench where revetting of footpath was continued.	

Army Form C. 2118.

WAR DIARY
or
INTELLIGENCE SUMMARY

(Erase heading not required.)

Instructions regarding War Diaries and Intelligence Summaries are contained in F. S. Regs., Part II. and the Staff Manual respectively. Title Pages will be prepared in manuscript.

Place	Date	Hour	Summary of Events and Information	Remarks and references to Appendices
A9, F, 82,	16/5/16	12 P.M.	General training carried on at A9, F, 8, 2. The two companies billeted at H, 5, Central marches to C,2,C, about central under Key billeted for the night.	
M,11, 6, 64	19/5/16	10 P.M.	Two companies and transport marched from A,9, F, 2 to M,17, 6, 64; the two companies billeted at C,2,C, together came the remainder of the Battalion paraded by the whole battalion was encamped by 5 P.M.	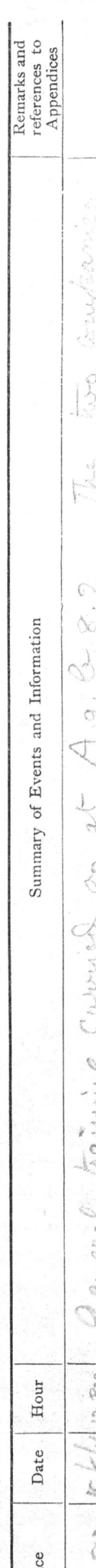
M,17, 6, 64	20/5/16	6 P.M.	Three officers reported to R.E. officers in the morning at 10 A.M. in order to look over some work for night 20/21 Two Companies carried out training in Camp & July Ry.	
M,17, 6, 64	21/5/16	6 P.M.	Two Companies supplied parties for work in front line trenches requiring letter supplied parties at N,18,c. Sandbagging were carried out night 28/21 at N,24,e, and N,18,c. & new lines.	
M,17, 6, 64	22/5/16	6 P.M.	Two Companies continues general training in Camp. The other two continued improving of front line trenches at N,24,c. after two continued improving of front line were ready for the winter on night 21/22. N,18,c. Sandbags only were used.	
M,17, 6, 64	23/5/16	6 P.M.	Two Companies continued repairing to sandbag & the front line trenches at N,24,c. and N,18,c. on night 22/23. The	

WAR DIARY or INTELLIGENCE SUMMARY

Army Form C. 2118.

(Erase heading not required.)

Place	Date	Hour	Summary of Events and Information	Remarks and references to Appendices
M.17, 6,4.	23/5/16	6 P.M.	Battalion marched out of Camp at M.17, 6, 6, 4 at 1 P.M. and reached the Camp at M, 6, d. at 2 P.M. and was encamped by 4 P.M. Two Companies were detailed for work on Reserve Trenches at N, 11, central.	
M, 6, d.	24/5/16	6 P.M.	Two Companies continued training in Camp(?) and the remaining Two supplied working parties for Reserve Trenches at N, 11, Central on night 23/24. Parapets were revetted with Sand-bags, and the continuation of trench was drawn and Carries on(?) of U frames and widening of trench was also carried out. Entrance of trench expanded were further convoyed to concealed from enemy's view. Two Companies continued training in Camp, the remaining two supplying parties for work at N,11 central, except with carried out also Sand-bagging and revetting as well a party of men also worked at 42 Trench ws & 2 required sand-bagging and revetting.	
M, 6, d.	25/5/16	6 A.M.		
M, 6, d.	26/5/16	6 P.M.	Two Companies continued training in camp till mid-day. Orders were then received for one section continuing to do emergency repairing of damage to front line trench	

WAR DIARY / INTELLIGENCE SUMMARY

Army Form C. 2118.

Place	Date	Hour	Summary of Events and Information	Remarks and references to Appendices
M,6,d,	26/5/16	6 P.M.	The remaining Companies continued deepening and widening support trench at N.11 central night 25/5/26, where work of sand-bagging and revetting of T heads was also continued.	
M,6,d,	27/5/16	6 P.M.	One Company began in camp the ordinary syllabus of trench (Part IV) work. 26/5/27 or for the three (heads) repairs (damage caused by previous heavy rain, mortar, at N.18 a were used for revetting, obstructions were laid). Sand-bags only were used for revetting. Obstructions were laid. At N.11 central the Companies of war commenced, and widening of support trenches continued (revetting, draining) and T heads.	
M,6,d,	28/5/16	6 P.M.	The following message was received from the 6th Division:— "I shall be much obliged if you will kindly convey to the Officer Commanding 20th K.R.R. on the 26th May with regard to the work done by that Battalion while to the excellent work done by that Battalion" The 6th Division employed under the orders of the 6th Division. The following message was received through the 20 E. and 3rd Divisional Headquarters:— "May 9 28th all ranks from — During the	

WAR DIARY or INTELLIGENCE SUMMARY

(Erase heading not required.)

Army Form C. 2118.

Place	Date	Hour	Summary of Events and Information	Remarks and references to Appendices
M.6.d.	28/9/16	6 PM	Rested in Camp. During night 27/28 One company continued repair work in front line trench at N.18, a portion of the repairs executed the previous night has to be done again owing to enemy artillery activity. Sand bags were continued and a number of U frames were also placed in position. Two more companies continued sand-bagging framing and revetting work on the support trench and T heads at N.11 Central.	
M.6.d.	29/9/16	6 PM	Two Companies (Cain's) on general training (i.e. after six nights of working parties) night 28/29 four work on support trench and T heads at N.11 Central. Revetting was done, trench and U frames were fixed, sandbags were filled (laced) and U frames were set and shoulders of T heads were entered in position and revetting and general training in camp for them two companies carried on.	
M.6.d.	30/9/16	6 PM	Two continued during night 29/30 with [illeg] revetting and drainage support trench and T heads at N.11 Central.	
M.6.d.	1/9/16	6 PM	Two companies carried on general training in camp. The remaining two supplied working parties on support trench and T heads at N.11 Central. Sandbag framing and drainage was [done]	

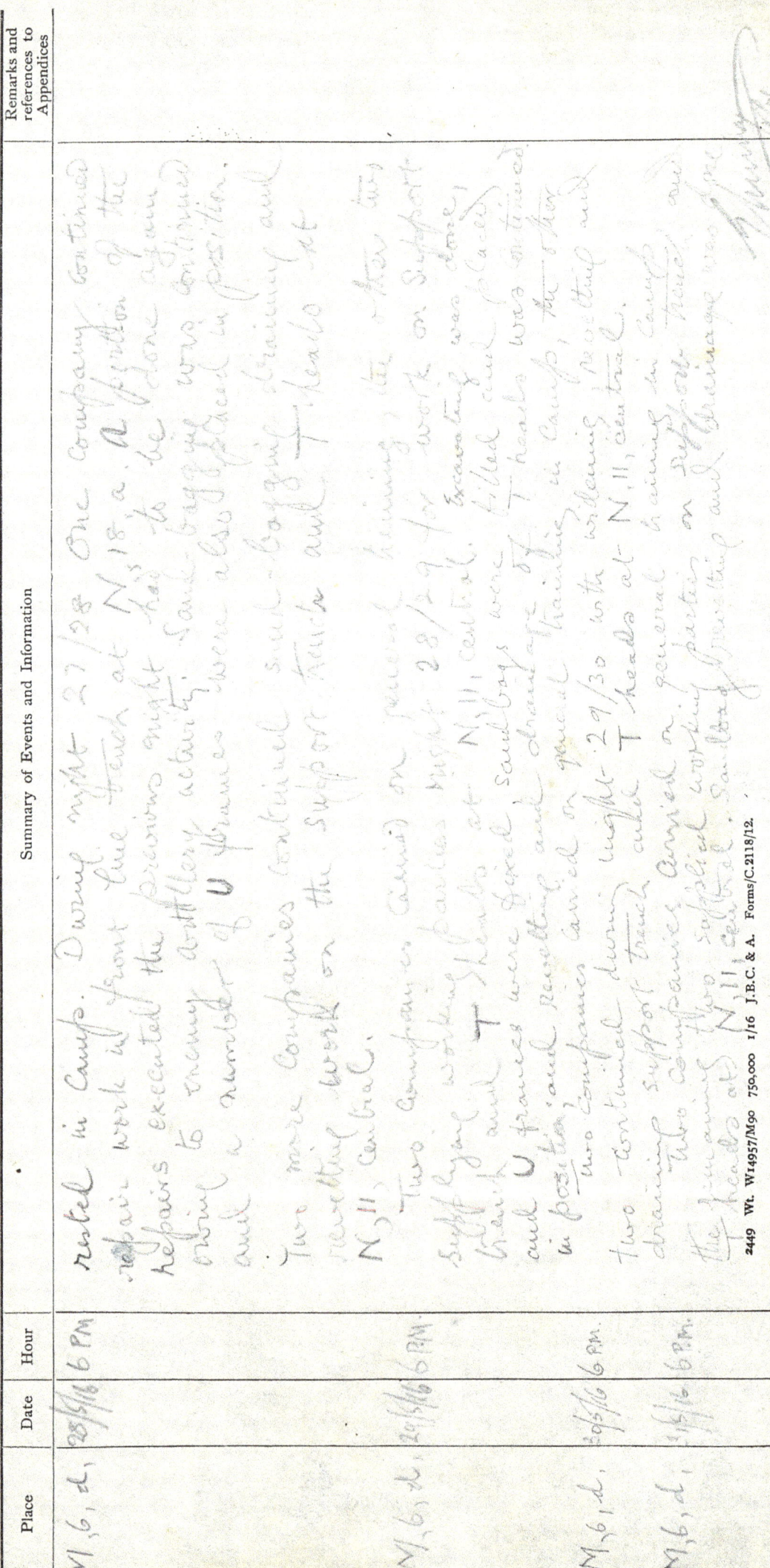

20 KRRC
vol 3
June

II

Confidential

War Diary
of
(signature) Brapini:

from 1st June 1916 to 30th June 1916.

Volume 3.

WAR DIARY or INTELLIGENCE SUMMARY

Army Form C. 2118.

Place	Date	Hour	Summary of Events and Information	Remarks and references to Appendices
M.6.d.	1/6/16	6 P.M.	Two Companies carried on training in camp, the remaining two continuing work on support trench and T heads at N.11. central.	
M.6.d.	2/6/16	6 P.M.	Two Companies trained in camp, the other two carrying on work at N.11. central night 1/2.	
M.6.d.	3/6/16	6 P.M.	Two companies (same) in camp, the remaining two continuing work at N.11. central on support trench and T heads night 2/3	
M.6.d.	4/6/16	6 P.M.	Two companies trained in camp, the other two carrying on with work at N.11. central on support trench & T heads, night 3/4	
M.6.d.	5/6/16	6 P.M.	Two Companies trained in camp, the other two carrying on work at N.11. central on support trench and T heads night 4/5	
M.6.d.	6/6/16	6 P.M.	Three companies carried out work on support trench & T heads at N.11. central, the fourth company supplying carrying party at N.5, d, 7, 8. night 5/6.	
M.6.d.	7/6/16	6 P.M.	Three companies carried out work on support trench and T heads, the fourth Company supplying party for new trench at N.5, d, 7, 8. night 6/7.	
M.6.d.	8/6/16	6 P.M.	Three companies continued work on support trench and T heads at N.11 central, the 4th Company worked at N.5, d, 7, 8. night 7/8.	

Army Form C. 2118.

WAR DIARY
or
INTELLIGENCE SUMMARY

(Erase heading not required.)

Instructions regarding War Diaries and Intelligence Summaries are contained in F.S. Regs., Part II. and the Staff Manual respectively. Title Pages will be prepared in manuscript.

Place	Date	Hour	Summary of Events and Information	Remarks and references to Appendices
M.6.d.	9/6/16	6 P.M.	Three companies continued work on support trench at N.11 central, nwetted, digging and sandbagging. The 4th Company working at N.5.a.7.4. night 8/9.	Reference N.5.D. sheet 57.d.S.E.
M.6.d.	10/6/16	6 P.M.	Three Companies carried on work of digging and revetting the support trench at N.11 central. The 4th Company continued the same class of work along a trench ※N.5.d. a continuous line being dug at right angles between the two map references. night 9/10	
M.6.d.	11/6/16	6 P.M.	Three Companies continued revetting and U framing and revetting support trench at N.11 central. The fourth Company carrying on with similar work at N.5.d. night 10/11 (drawing shown)	
M.6.d.	12/6/16	6 PM	Three Companies continued revetting at N.11 central and N.11.B. necessary. The support trench at N.11 C. the fourth Company was told on to add on to support trench N.5.d. and work on continuing work on support night 11/12	
M.6.d.	13/6/16	6.P.M.	Three Companies continued revetting support trench N.11 central & N.11 B. support trench heavy N.11 central to N.5.d. fourth Company continued strutting revetting at N.5.d.	

WAR DIARY
or
INTELLIGENCE SUMMARY

Army Form C. 2118.

Place	Date	Hour	Summary of Events and Information	Remarks and references to Appendices
M,6,d,	13/6/16	6 P.M.	Three companies supplied working parties to continue revetting and draining where necessary along trench N.11, central, — to — N,5,d,. The fourth Company started a new fire trench commencing at N,17, d, 5,6, running in an Easterly direction to S.N. 17,b. Wiring two stated companies with both the digging. night 12/13	
M,6,d	14/6/16	6 P.M.	Three companies continues revetting and draining new trench, and draining on support trench at N.11 central — N,11, b, and N,5,d,3, The fourth Company continuing wiring and construction of new trench at N,17,a, and N,17,6, night 13/14	
M,6,d,	15/6/16	6 P.M.	Three companies continued digging trench, with including drainage U draining revetting and digging a former Pit in support trench at N,11 central, N,11,b, and N,5,d, The fourth Company continuing wiring and digging at N,17,a, to night 14/15	

Army Form C. 2118.

WAR DIARY
or
INTELLIGENCE SUMMARY
(Erase heading not required.)

Place	Date	Hour	Summary of Events and Information	Remarks and references to Appendices
M.6.d.	14/1/16	6 P.M.	Three companies continued W strengthening drainage support trench at M11 and S M11 C 2 & N5d, the fourth company continued work on new keep at N11 d & c, material being carried up gradually. Hostile shell - unmerciful about M11 d 15 & New keep.	
N.5.d, M.6.d	15/1/16	6 P.M.	One company at N.5.d fixed U frames, revetted with expanded metal and carried material to break to Brewsworth was put into course of construction & duties of accumulation of water in original trench owing to ... Another company at N.3.b. revetted with expanded metal and U frames a section of the french lines widened & deepened, and the parados was strengthened for some distance. Another company worked on break at N.11 central, also fixed U frames and expanded metal for new parapet & placed in position sandbags where necessary. Night 15/17	
M.6.d	18/1/16	6 P.M.	One company continued widening french trench toward N.5.d & other trenches expanded metal and bank boards at N.5.d. Another company at N.11 & N.11 & 5 revetted front french with sandbags and carried at N.11 & 5.	

WAR DIARY
or
INTELLIGENCE SUMMARY

Army Form C. 2118.

Place	Date	Hour	Summary of Events and Information	Remarks and references to Appendices
M, 6, d.	18/6/16	6 P.M.	Material from Dumps to trench. Another company continued to dig a third trench, carried up material and erected barbed wire entanglements at N,11, a, 6. The fourth company continued fixing up V frames at N,11 central night 17/18 continued fixing up V frames for work at N,5, d, own suspended. The company on	
M, 6, d.	19/6/16	6 P.M.	that area took over work with another company on support trench at N,11, b. At this section of the new trench. Two companies worked on sand bag revetment and Pump another company continued revetting and fix up V continued fixing up V frames dug latrines and Pumped water out of the trench. The fourth company at N,11 central. The fourth company fix up V frames at N,11 central; continued wiring and digging a new trench. N,11, a, 6. night 18/19	
M, 6, d.	20/6/16	6 P.M.	Two Companies continued work of revetting, fixing V frames and sandbagging in support trench at N,11, b. The third Company continued similar work at N,11 central, while the fourth Company erected more wire entanglement any	

Place	Date	Hour	Summary of Events and Information	Remarks and references to Appendices
M.6.d.	20/6/16	6pm	Continued digging dug-outs and steps (W) framing Hut Park Blandery dug. night 19/20	
M.6.d.	21/6/16	6pm	One Company took on work again at N.5.d. Supplying labour for the three, and at N.11.b. Another Company at N.11.b. (continued) fixing W frames and expanded Donetal (northern Enougther U frames) at N.11. central continued work & fixing sills & rails ; the fourth Company at N.17.a.& carried on with timber, digging and U framing. Night 20/21	
M.6.d.	22/6/16	6pm	One Company supplied working parties as more at N.5.d. and N.11.b. Another Company working at the two points; supplying it for brickwork being done at the latter point ; another Company working at was carried out N.5.d. Another Company working at N.11.b. fixed U frames, revetted and completed laking N.11. b. Another Company continued fixing W frames French frames and expanded metra at N.11 central, the fourth	

Army Form C. 2118.

WAR DIARY or INTELLIGENCE SUMMARY

(Erase heading not required.)

Place	Date	Hour	Summary of Events and Information	Remarks and references to Appendices
M.6.d.	22/8/16	6 P.M.	Company paraded and marched up to trench to resume U frames and continued erection of barbed wire entanglement. Night 21/22	
M.6.d.	23/8/16	6 P.M.	One company arrived on with wire work at N.5.d. and fixed U frames. Expended metal at N.11.b. Rest where another company continued putting up Expanded metal (for purpose of camouflage) barbed wire also fixed in position. U frames being fixed in position. At N.11 Central, another company continued erection of deepened communication and fixed trench boyto. The fourth company continued at N.17.a.b. with digging new trench in preparation for U framing. Night 22/23	
M.6.d.	24/8/16	6 P.M.	One company carried on with revetting, U framing and Expanded metal at N.5.d., and fixed U frames and Expanded metal at N.11.b. At the point another company continued as usual with U framing and revetting.	

WAR DIARY
or
INTELLIGENCE SUMMARY

Army Form C. 2118.

Place	Date	Hour	Summary of Events and Information	Remarks and references to Appendices
M.16.a.	24/8/16	1 P.M.	and nailing down new boards. Another working party at N.11 authorized fixed (?) frames. Heavy hostile shelling early morning and evening M. 16. a. and central M.17. a. severed telephone communication French and Bn. H.Q. Line to left company crater (more traffic) were extensively damaged — 24 craters 23/24 debris and fuel (more U/[unclear] mines at N.17.a. M.16. 23/24 ... One Company continued trench work at M.5. and also completed Revetting (?) parapet/push at N.5. and M.11.b. and the company working at this (?) part of trench gelled small(?) and (?) expanded metal revetment. Another Company finished at (?) cut-furnishing at T.15.g.h. upon reinforcement trench N.11. central. The fourth Company (?) the grave(?) was entrenchment(?) draining French communication trench and grave(?) Bryonies at M.17.a.b. M.9.c. 24/25	

WAR DIARY or INTELLIGENCE SUMMARY

Army Form C. 2118.

Place	Date	Hour	Summary of Events and Information	Remarks and references to Appendices
M.6.d.	26/8/16	6 P.M.	One Company continued revetment of trench at N.11.b. and topsods breastwork at N.5.a. Another Company engaged with sandbagging, draining and drainage of trench also at N.11.b. Another Company at N.11. central continued finishing revetment of a section of trench complete & training in another section. The fourth Company fixed U frames, drainers trench and erected more wire entanglement at N.17.a.b. night 25/26. Booth impossible owing to exceptionally bad weather night 26/27.	
M.6.d.	27/8/16			
M.6.d.	28/8/16	6 P.M.	One Company continued to complete revetment of trench at N.11.b. and fixed U frames and continued with parapet and trench at N.5.b. Another Company drained trench and worked on with revetment at N.11.b. (N.11.b. about central.) Another Company fixed more U frames and erected more wire entanglement at N.17.a.b. The fourth Company worked out new continuation of N.11.b. night 27/28.	

J Brown

Army Form C. 2118.

WAR DIARY
INTELLIGENCE SUMMARY
(Erase heading not required.)

Place	Date	Hour	Summary of Events and Information	Remarks and references to Appendices
M.6.d	29/6/16	6 P.m.	One Company continued with the bombard construction at N.5.d. Another Company draining and revetting at M.11.c. The third Company worked on trench N.11 central & N.11.d in Squ 28/29	
M.6.d	30/6/16	1 P.m.	One Company returned revetment trench at N.11.c.(III) One Company continued with development at N.5.d. Another Company continued with drainage and revetting in trench at N.11.c. Carried boards expanded metal etc. were issued at N.11. Trench boards expanded metal & etc were issued. The work continued in front central & another buttress before M.11.a.6. While 29/30 v premium and showering	
M.6.d				

Pioneers.
3rd Div.

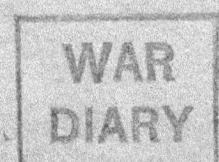

20th BATTN. THE KING'S ROYAL RIFLE CORPS.

J U L Y

1 9 1 6

INTELLIGENCE SUMMARY

(Erase heading not required.)

Instructions regarding War Diaries and Intelligence Summaries are contained in F.S. Regs., Part II. and the Staff Manual respectively. Title Pages will be prepared in manuscript.

Place	Date	Hour	Summary of Events and Information	Remarks and references to Appendices
M.6.d.	1/7/16	6 P.M.	One Company continues marching [illegible] at N5b [illegible] north [illegible] Another company [illegible] and section started [illegible] and section [illegible] [illegible] continued working and [illegible] 30/1 Orders received [illegible] to work on S.W. [illegible] returned.	
M.6.d.	2/7/16	9 P.M.	One Company left M.6.d. to entrain at 7.30 P.M. for 45 Army Area. H.Q.S. wagons also left camp for same destination.	
M.6.d.	3/7/16	9 P.M.	The remainder of the battalion with all transport left M.6.d. by tram at 9.15 a.m. reaching Littlewarne station. A's Company entrained by 7.30 P.M. when the other detachments were arranged with the [illegible] men in station. This company with the [illegible] marched to [illegible] where the remainder billeted in barns near detachments station.	+train left [illegible] arrived [illegible] [illegible] at Sylvain [illegible]
✳	4/7/16	2 P.M.	The remainder of the battalion marched next morning at 7.30 a.m. reaching [illegible] transport at 2 P.M. & [illegible] was	

INTELLIGENCE SUMMARY

(Erase heading not required.)

Instructions regarding War Diaries and Intelligence Summaries are contained in F. S. Regs., Part II. and the Staff Manual respectively. Title Pages will be prepared in manuscript.

Place	Date	Hour	Summary of Events and Information	Remarks and references to Appendices
✱	4/7/16	12 P.m.	made here, the whole battalion marching on again at 7.30 P.m., reaching its next destination at 11.30 P.m., ~~marching~~ bivouacing where billets were obtained for all.	✱ No map reference possible
✱	5/7/16	12 P.m.	At 4 P.m. An advance party left in 1 motor lorry for new camp area and included officers to look over new work. At 5 P.m. 2½ Companies followed in motor buses for same destination, under charge of 2nd in command. The transport this Bn. Party left at 11.30 P.m. arriving about midnight. The remaining 1½ Companies & transport mules Coy officers marched out at 7.30 P.m., and reached a village at midnight where they bivouaced in an orchard.	✱ 5 Squared map.
✱	6/7/16	10.30 P.m.	The 1½ Companies & transport mules Coy Officer marched out at 9.30 P.m. to meet up in rear of Brigade and follow it to the next billets, place for billets was at [?]	
✱	7/7/16	10.30 P.m.	The 1½ Companies under Coy Officer arrived in billets soon after mid-day. A message was received till after mid-day. A message arrived at 9.0 A.m., but no further orders arrived. The Companies then [?] them billets for the night. ½ Coy Officer dismissed the [?]	
+ A.14.a	8/7/16	12 P.m.	One and a half Companies carried working material to [forward] dumps & bridges which they remaining 2½ Companies continued making roads & bridges on the 6th & 7th July. started on the 6th July.	+ Ref map MONTAUBAN

INTELLIGENCE SUMMARY

(Erase heading not required.)

Place	Date	Hour	Summary of Events and Information	Remarks and references to Appendices
A.14.a	9/7/16	12 P.M.	The Battalion split into parties already referred to worked throughout day & night on road - making, wire-pulling and collecting material. The troops being organised into squads worked with.	
A.14.a	10/7/16 12 P.M.		The Battalion continued work throughout day.	
A.14.a	11/7/16 12 P.M.		Enemy shelling was advanced on several points.	
A.14.a	12/7/16 12 P.M.		Brig- Sullivan inspected work and arrived at 11.0 [?] and [?]. Battalion rested after full day's work at [?] Peter sector.	
A.14.a	13/7/16 12 P.M.		Party to work in two shifts (teams) of 5 hr, one taking up assembly position [?] 5.15 & there for two hours. 11 P.M. for two hours return. The party at 5.15 went out of the trenches and were relieved about 7 P.M. the party at 8.15 were out in trenches about 10 o'clock.	
A.14.a	15/7/16 12 P.M.		Work was carried on as at 5/6 but omitted and Sibles from the commencement of daytime, the parties no longer using the [?] and [?] but keeping [?] and [?] afternoon of the 75th inst.	
A.14.a	16/7/16 12 P.M.		Work was continued at 5.15 night when and 8.15 the latter strong point will only be dealt with at night.	

2449 Wt. W14957/Mg0 750,000 1/16 J.B.C. & A. Forms/C.2118/12.

INTELLIGENCE SUMMARY

(Erase heading not required.)

Place	Date	Hour	Summary of Events and Information	Remarks and references to Appendices
A.14.a.	17/7/16	12 P.M.	Work of consolidating at S.15, about central was continued during the day, while the Company in bivouac at S.22.c.5.6. continued work consolidation of Strong point around & Communication trenches at S.16.b. During night 17/18, the Company last relieved from posts at S.15. about central (C.15 and 7 Raid) done some road work daily from the 16th inst., was sent up to S.21.d.1.5. await the orders of the 76th Brigade, and it remained there all day and night 18/19.	
A.14.a.	18/7/16 12 P.M.		The consolidation of area at S.15 about central was continued until 12 noon 18th inst., when the other two Companies at (work) camp and bivouac (sig.) 18.1.1.1 the Company returned to camp, and all our consolidated communication trenches with those consolidated upon [to camp]. Those companies Company engaged at S.15. was recalled to camp. Those continuing work at S.22.c.5.8. was recalled to the (reform) of continuing road officers were to 7th drawn for the reform of the 76th Brigade road	
A.14.a.	19/7/15 12 P.M.		The Company awaiting orders of the 76th Brigade bivouacs. During Sent back to camp and arrived during the afternoon. During the evening, one Company was ordered to proceed to	

INTELLIGENCE SUMMARY.

(Erase heading not required.)

Place	Date	Hour	Summary of Events and Information	Remarks and references to Appendices
A.14.a	19/7/16	12P.M.	S.17, c.6.3. to dig a fire trench. This company dug 80 yards of fire trench and cleared C.T. from S.17. c.6.3 to S.17. c.3.1. The work was much interfered with by heavy shell fire. E.F.	
A.14.a.	20/7/16	12P.M.	1.0 A.M. the fire was so heavy that it became impossible for the Company to carry on & Camp at 2.15 a.m. 20th July. At 4.30 a.m. orders were received for 2 Companies to proceed as soon as possible to consolidate west of east side of White Crater situated at S.17.b. They left Camp with material in limbers at 6.45 a.m. As soon as information being received to the effect that work was not possible, the 2 Companies were recalled by C.O. at 12 noon and arrived Camp having been at S.17, c.2.8. 9.1.5.7. They had successfully carried materiel to S.17, c.2.6. but had been obliged to return to S.22.C.8.7. On the advice of G.O.C. 76 Brigade, the two Companies were brought back to Camp, arriving there at 1.30 P.M. During the	

INTELLIGENCE SUMMARY

(Erase heading not required.)

Place	Date	Hour	Summary of Events and Information	Remarks and references to Appendices
A.14.a.	20/7/16	12 P.M.	morning that other two Companies worked at road repairs, during the afternoon and night 20/21 all Companies rested.	
A.14.a.	21/7/16	8 P.M.	Two Companies left Camp to work on trench at S.17.c. and the other two left at the same time for work at S.18.c.	
A.14.a.	22/7/16	10 A.M.	The two Companies working near S.17.c. and S.17.c.i.i. covered a certain amount of wiring material and some wiring and dug a part of existing trench. The Karafsot very held up and all work has been much impeded by very heavy shell fire. The other two Companies did Opn. work at S.18.c. began forward from getting to work owing to heavy shell fire which prevented them transport from reaching the appointed Dumps. The enemy artillery were particularly active that night, 21/22. The Companies returned to Camp during early hours of the morning.	

INTELLIGENCE SUMMARY

(Erase heading not required.)

Place	Date	Hour	Summary of Events and Information	Remarks and references to Appendices
A.14.a.	23/7/16	8 p.m.	On night 22/23 one company dug a trench from S.18.a.7.4. to S.18. central. This trench was not quite completed owing to several casualties being received while the company was on its way up to work.	
			Two companies left camp at 2 p.m. to await orders of 9th Brigade at S.22.d.2.6. At 3 p.m. orders were received for all four companies to report in Tom Trench at S.18.c.0.10, S.24.b.9.9, and S.18.c.2.4. to S.18.c. central. The two companies from camp came up in time awaiting relief of 9th Brigade did not arrive until completely wiring for about 3/4 of distance at 3.30	
A.14.a.	24/7/16	5 a.m.	A.M. 24/7/16	
A.14.a.	25/7/16	5 a.m.	During night 24/25 parties were sent up again to complete wiring in front of this trench from S.17.c.6.4 to S.23.b.10.8. They succeeded in wiring 350 yds but were held up on that wiring owing to heavy shell fire	

INTELLIGENCE SUMMARY.
(Erase heading not required.)

Place	Date	Hour	Summary of Events and Information	Remarks and references to Appendices
A.14.a	25/7/16	5 A.m.	Two other parties were sent to dig a trench at S.24.a.9.9. and to complete wiring at S.18.d.1.1. These parties were obliged to stand to under orders of nearest infantry officers owing to counter attack on the part of the enemy. These parties returned to camp at 3 a.m.	
*				* Ref. Map. Sheet 62D. N.E. France
K.2.d.6.3.	25/7/16	8 P.m.	The battalion left camp at A.14.a. at 2 P.m. and were encamped at K.2.d.6.3. by 7 P.m. The battalion rested all day.	
K.2.d.6.3.	26/7/16	8 P.m.		
K.2.d.6.3.	27/7/16	8 P.m.	The companies spent the morning bathing and rested by remainder of the day except for one hour physical drill and kit inspection	
K.2.d.6.3.	28/7/16	8 P.m.	The companies spent the morning at squad & physical drill and bathing.	
K.2.d.6.3. J.5.a.8.3.	29/7/16 30/7/16	8 P.m. 8 P.m.	The same programme was carried out during the morning. The battalion left camp at 10 a.m. and were bivouacced at J.5.a.1.8. by 12 noon	

Place	Date	Hour	Summary of Events and Information	Remarks and references to Appendices
J.5.a.8.8.	31/9/16	6 P.M.	The battalion did physical and squad drill during the morning. Inspection of kit and rifles was held by company Officers and 2 drums afternoon.	

Yeo Henry Lt Col
3/9/16

3rd Divisional Troops

20th BATTALION

KING'S ROYAL RIFLE CORPS (Pioneers)

AUGUST 1 9 1 6

From:- O.C., 20th K.R.R.C.
To:- "Q" Office, 3rd Division.

Herewith War Diary for period 1st to 31st August 1916.

Thos Funnell M/Capt
for Lt. Colonel
Comdg. 20th (S) Bn. K.R.R. Corps
(Pioneers)

In the Field.
5.9.16.

WAR DIARY
or
INTELLIGENCE SUMMARY

Army Form C. 2118.

Instructions regarding War Diaries and Intelligence Summaries are contained in F.S. Regs., Part II. and the Staff Manual respectively. Title pages will be prepared in manuscript.

(Erase heading not required.)

Place	Date	Hour	Summary of Events and Information	Remarks and references to Appendices
J.5.a.8.8.	1/8/16	8 P.M.	Training in camp carried on during the morning including physical drill and squad drill.	
J.5.a.8.8.	2/8/16	1 P.M.	Physical training & squad drill during the morning. The battalion did a route march in the evening to D.15.c. Central via D, Squares 29, 23, 16 and 15, returning by D, Squares 15, 21, 27, 28, and 29.	
J.5.a.8.8.	3/8/16	12 P.M.	The usual training programme carried out during the morning. In the evening the battalion practiced consolidation of ground at J.11.b. and J.12.a. Officers and N.C.Os instructed work done overnight consolidating strong points. The usual training programme being carried out in camp under C.O. C.Q.S.	
		6 P.M.	Orders received from Coys H.Q. for his Companies to be ready to move on receipt of further orders to forward area for defence works under instruction of C.R.E.	
		12 P.M.	At 8.15 P.M. 2 Companies carried out concentration march	

WAR DIARY
or
INTELLIGENCE SUMMARY.
(Erase heading not required.)

Army Form C. 2118.

Instructions regarding War Diaries and Intelligence Summaries are contained in F. S. Regs., Part II. and the Staff Manual respectively. Title pages will be prepared in manuscript.

Place	Date	Hour	Summary of Events and Information	Remarks and references to Appendices
J.5,a,8.8	4/8/16	12 P.M.	acting as fire companies. Companies concentrated between 10 P.M. & 10.30 P.M. at J.18,12,24,81. Companies arrived back in camp by 11.30 P.M.	
J.5,a,8.8	5/8/16	12 P.M.	Two Companies carried out physical training and wiring practice. The right half battalion marched out of camp at 4.45 P.M. and reached forward camp at F.16,c, at 8.15 P.M.	
J.5,a,8.8	6/8/16	4 P.M.	Left half battalion rested all day in camp. At F.16.c. Limbers were prepared for wiring material for the right half battalion.	
J.5,a,8.8	7/8/16	4 P.M.	The left half battalion carried out general training. The first working party from #F.16.c. left the camp at 5 P.M. 6/8/16, to work at S.2.g. about central. The parties worked forward another from the lose schemes of the new strench that had to be wired. The parties gave male from two pickets of each company in the right half battalion. Two rows of pickets were	

T.2134. Wt. W708—776. 500000. 4/15. Sir J. C. & S.

Place	Date	Hour	Summary of Events and Information	Remarks and references to Appendices
T.5, a, 8, 8.	7/8/16	4 p.m.	put out for a distance of 300 yds, and this was partially wired. Further 40 yds was completed. Wires and in addition, 50 yds of single line of pickets driven was laid down. In accordance with orders from BUGLE 10 men were detailed from C.Coy at F.16.C. to be at Coy. B at 7 a.m. for special work. There was considerable shell fire during the time the parties were working at the wiring.	
T.5, a, 8, 8	8/8/16	6.10 p.m.	The left half battalion carried on with the general training including wiring, physical drill and bayonet fighting. The right half battalion at F.16.C, sent up working parties 7/8/16 before wiring was completed in front of trench from S.28.c.5.1. to S.28.d.1.4.2, while two rows of wire were put in from S.28.d.1.4.2, to A.4.b.5.5. (Ref map MONTAUBAN SHEET) at 11.58 p.m. the 2nd in Command (O.C. Detachment at F.16.C.) received orders to withdraw all working parties and to send no more until further orders. During morning of 8/8/16 the right half battalion did physical drill, and inspected rifles etc. pending further orders being received.	

WAR DIARY or INTELLIGENCE SUMMARY

(Erase heading not required.)

Army Form C. 2118.

Instructions regarding War Diaries and Intelligence Summaries are contained in F.S. Regs., Part II. and the Staff Manual respectively. Title pages will be prepared in manuscript.

Place	Date	Hour	Summary of Events and Information	Remarks and references to Appendices
J.5.a.8.8.	8/8/16	6.15 p.m.	The left half battalion left camp for route march to J.29.c.3.7. returning to camp at 9.15 p.m.	
J.5.a.8.8.	9/8/16	12 noon	The left ½ battalion carried out general training in physical drill, arms drill, and wiring during the morning. On the afternoon of 8/8/16 working parties of F.16.c. were able in spite of being strongly shelled & fired at from long range, were from the BRIQUETERIE defence. 6 A.5.8.6.3. Three companies were clearing light front & communication trenches. Through careful handling by officers in charge and being humanely caused. A report from Col. Ozeran in charge, stated that it was difficult to get reliefs up to the line & stressed it had been possible to keep the companies supplied. The first in relief was at F.16.C. at 12.30 a.m. on 9/8/16.	
J.5.a.8.8.	10/8/16	7 p.m.	The left ½ Battalion carried out several training in camp, its hours being altered owing to wet weather. 1 Company went	

WAR DIARY or INTELLIGENCE SUMMARY

Place	Date	Hour	Summary of Events and Information	Remarks and references to Appendices
J.5,a,8,c.	10/8/16	9 P.m.	For a Route march in the evening. The other remaining ½ Company (besides ½ to marching next morning) ½ F.16.c. for the purpose of relieving a Company at work on wiring. The Companies at F.16.c. continued wiring on the line from S.28.c. to A.5.b. The wiring being increased to four rows, with an addition in front of triangular wiring facing the enemy during 9th August.	
J.5,a,8,8.	11/8/16	10 A.m. 9 P.m.	One Company of the left half Battalion left at 9.30 A.m. for F.16.c. (arrived in the afternoon). The remaining Company and Transport left J.5,a,8,8, at 4 Pm arriving F.13, b, 9.9. at 7 P.m. Headquarters left with that Company. Wiring during the 10th Aug. The Companies at F.16.c. continued wiring during the 10th Aug. One Company being relieved at F.16.c. marched to F.13, b,9,9. the Company already there moved to F.16.c. to relieve the 2nd Company which had been wiring at S.28.c. During the 11th Aug wiring was completed in the right sector of the line.	
F.13,b,9,9.	12/8/16	6 P.m.		

WAR DIARY
or
INTELLIGENCE SUMMARY

Army Form C. 2118.

(Erase heading not required.)

Instructions regarding War Diaries and Intelligence Summaries are contained in F. S. Regs., Part II. and the Staff Manual respectively. Title Pages will be prepared in manuscript.

Place	Date	Hour	Summary of Events and Information	Remarks and references to Appendices
F.15.c.9.8.	13/8/16	6 P.M.	The 2nd Company to be relieved at F.16.c. remains in camp at F.15.b.9.9. to relieve 2nd Coy. the 13th Aug. further work 1000 feet in on the left sector (the quality & distance of 200 yards were wiring also suitably constituted. The covering consisted where complete of hyp. 2nd Coy wire work a triangular fence. 30 layer low bunn & plan switching were secured. Work to cease will the 15P. mere Instruction to prepare to start with next day during the 6 hour shifts commencing around the 10th moving in to deploy. Fronts at 100 ft each effect (as expressed into the 2 officers) the officers into the 2nd Army Place R.E.	
F.16.c.5.2./4.8/16	8 A.M.	The troops of Nos. 3 & 4 were moved from Camp to deploy at the Fed. Field Companies R.E. at 10.2 a.m. A look on dugouts at A.5.c.3.3. F.16.(Bay 13)K/16 the front line of Krinne pet infantry Durant the (with) from S.2.9.9. R.13 & nights in front of supplies (at F.16.d) also picking wire from S.2 & 4 & tunnels	
	10 P.M.	... Brigadiers: the work completed before the curtain at 4 M.A.	

WAR DIARY or INTELLIGENCE SUMMARY

Army Form C. 2118.

Place	Date	Hour	Summary of Events and Information	Remarks and references to Appendices
F.16,c,5,2	14/8/16	10 P.M.	The two Companies at F.13,b,7,9, marched to F.16,c,5,2, and were encamped by 5 P.M. Transport remained at F.13,b,7,9. A party was ordered to report to 183rd Tunnelling Company at F.11, central by 8 P.M. This was duly carried out under charge of 1 Officer and 140 men & 2 officers. Another fresh carrying party of 1 Officer and 30 men were ordered to Allouatter work on tramway. This was duly carried out. There report at Allouatter work on tramway and work parties Billeted at the area (work in both cases). There was no more wiring done that night. Rainie to cease after the night of 13th Aug. in order that new parties in All. be provided for min on dugouts at A,5,d,3,3. At 2 P.m. the 2nd relief of 100 men & 2 officers left Camp and took over at 4 P.m. from the 1st shift which returned to Camp at 6 P.m. At 8 P.m. the 3rd relief left Camp and took over from the 2nd relief at 10 P.m. This relief	
		12 P.M.	reached Camp at 12 midnight 14/8/16 took over work on dug-outs The fourth relief left Camp and	
F.11,b,c,5,2	15/8/16	2 A.M.	from 3rd relief at 4 A.m. at A,5,d,3,3, taking over at 4 to A.m. for work at dig outs at A.5,d,3,3, left Camp at 8 A.M. Orders were received at 12	
		12.30 P.M.	to 10 A.M. This was the last party of 67, as orders requiring the following noon, that as many men as possible we required (losing of line) from 5.30 L,7,6 to afternoon to assemble for consolidation (lining of line) were to be done by 15/8/16. B.1,d,7,8. The work on Hin Line was to be completed by 15/8/16. attack to be made by the 3rd Division on the afternoon of 15/8/16. An much excavation as possible had been	
		5.30 P.M.	The first relief returned to Camp. carried out under the R.E.s by the working parties engaged on the Dugouts.	

WAR DIARY
or
INTELLIGENCE SUMMARY

(Erase heading not required.)

Army Form C. 2118.

Place	Date	Hour	Summary of Events and Information	Remarks and references to Appendices
F,16,C,5,2,	15/8/16	11.40 PM	The following orders were received from 3rd Division relating to consolidation of line from S,30,b,7,2, to B,1,d,7,8. For the 76th Infantry Brigade: 80 men to construct S.P. at B,1,c,2,4, and 160 men to construct S.P. at B,1,d,2,6. For the 9th Brigade: 80 men to construct a Strong Point at T,25,b,8,9. The remainder of the Battalion to remain in Reserve in their billets ready to move at 15 minutes notice. (At 11th Aug 15th [illegible] 30 [illegible] were [illegible] to [illegible] different [illegible] with [illegible] Division from Asylum: 60 men were [illegible] to [illegible] [illegible] [illegible] started work.	
F,16,C,5,2,	16/8/16	10 AM	The path with the 183rd Tunnelling Company at F,11,6, [illegible] at A,5,d,7,9, on 15/8/16 R.E.'s at construction of dug outs [illegible] continue [illegible] some days. The officer in charge states in his report the work will [illegible] A,5,b,3 at 6 P.M. They 160 men & 3 officer left camp and reached A,5,b,3 at 6 P.M. They remained near by and awaited orders of 76th Brigade. The other party of 80 men and 2 officers left camp and reached same area at the same hour and awaited orders from 76th Brigade.	
		2 P.M.	The working party for 9th Brigade also left camp and marched A,3,4,1, at 4½ P.M. When they awaited orders. 7 officers went up in the morning to look over area near T,15,C,4,9, and reached A,3,d,3,1, at 5 P.M.	

Army Form C. 2118.

WAR DIARY
or
INTELLIGENCE SUMMARY
(Erase heading not required.)

Place	Date	Hour	Summary of Events and Information	Remarks and references to Appendices
F.16, c, 5, 2	17/8/16	12 noon	The working parties for the 76th Brigade remained all night near A.5, d, 3, 3, it having been impossible to dig any hole. The morning was spent in digging in. The working party for the 9th Brigade was also unable to do work, and remained at A.3, d, 0, 1, in trenches.	
		7 P.M.	The party with the 183rd Tunnelling Company at F.11, 2, central, reached camp, having received orders from the C.R.E. to keep shelter work at A.5, d, 7, 9, had not been possible during night 16/17.	
		7.30 R.M.	The party attached to 9th Brigade reached camp having received orders to return from A.3, d, 0, 1, through the 9th Brigade.	
		9.0 P.M.	Orders having been received from the C.R.E. to supply a working party of 2 officers & 100 N.C.O.s & men to proceed early next morning to ravine A.5, d, 7, 9, for the purpose of enlarging trench from avenue, there to A.6, a, 3, 9/0, the party was detrained from among those point up who had returned at 4 a.m. 18/8/16, the 183rd Tunnelling Company. Their orders were to leave camp at 4 a.m. 18/8/16. The working parties for the 76th Brigade continued to wait orders at A.5, d, 3, 3. They completed shelters at A.5, d, 4, 3, and strengthened & built half trench at B.1, c, 18, to strong point. 80 men were used on these two pieces of work. Another party of 60 men dug a traversed trench 140 yards long	

2449 Wt. W14957/M90 750,000 1/16 J.B.C. & A. Forms/C.2118/12.

WAR DIARY
or
INTELLIGENCE SUMMARY

Army Form C. 2118.

Place	Date	Hour	Summary of Events and Information	Remarks and references to Appendices
F,16,c,5,2,	17/8/16	10 P.M.	at A.6. about central. Another party 60 men started digging a trench near the same place. But little work was done owing to much rifle & machine gun fire.	
F,16,c,5,9,	18/8/16	10.15 AM	A party of 80 men and 2 officers left camp to meet the G.O.C. Brigade H.Q. at A.5.d.B.3 and await orders of G.O.C. 78 Brigade 78	
		6 P.M.	Orders were received from G.O.C. 78 Brigade to go and work in front of new trench. A party of 2 officers and 120 men went through B.1 square & no 5 C. Trench up on road through B.1 square & no 5 C. hours received at camp that the party detailed for work above mentioned to A.5.d.9.3. M.C.C. 76 Brigade was unable to work until returns from orders of Commander of 6260 & Newcomb. They were very heavy shell fire, and it was particularly unwise that one casualties was received while gathering from the trench. The party attended to by an Engineer Field Co. & returned to camp 86 men were sent up at 7 P.M. by 8 P.M. 18/19, but were not up at 7 A.M. 19 A.M.	
F,16,c,5,2,	19/8/16	8 A.M.	Six officers and 235 O.R. left camp after breakfast relieved the position there, was relieved to 6 F.S.C. 8. 9.	
		10 A.M.		
		8.45 P.M.	3 Th, The party of 2 officers and 80 men returned to camp under orders	

WAR DIARY
or
INTELLIGENCE SUMMARY

(Erase heading not required.)

Army Form C. 2118.

Place	Date	Hour	Summary of Events and Information	Remarks and references to Appendices
F.16,c,5,2.	19/8/16	8.45 P.m.	of the 9th Brigade. This party had worked on clearing and widening the trench for 300 yards at about S.30,c,7,2, work commenced at 7a.m. ceasing at 11.30 a.m. The men resumed work at 1 P.m. finally leaving off at 5.30 P.m. Thus 9 hours were put in altogether, and the result was very satisfactory, because it enabled troops to (one one man for in the trench. Provision to turn the extreme naturness of the trench made it difficult to even one stream of traffic. This fault exists at present in many of the trenches in that area, and it is quite impossible under such circumstances without a good carry out relieving of troops without confusion & delay and releases during 19/20, but 6 officers and 235 O.R. The Division was released in dug outs at A.5, d, h, 3.	
F.16,c,5,2.	20/8/16	11 A.M.	still remained in dug outs at A.5, d, h, 3. 2 N.C.O's and 11 men returned to Camp. Work under Officer i/c Divisional Dump. 1 Officer and 30 other ranks detailed for work on maintenance of tramway at A.14, Central, returned to camp. They went out at 2.35 O.R. returned to camp at 1 A.m., work lasted from 6.15 A.m to 5 A.m.	
		12 A.M.	The party consisting of 1 officer and 30 other ranks detailed for work on maintenance of tramway at A.14, Central, returned to camp.	
		1.15 P.m.	The party of 6 officers and 235 O.R. lent to 76th Brigade as a C.T. about 250 yards long to a depth of 5'6" to work for 76th Brigade. This party consisted in digging a C.T. about 250 yards long to a depth of 5'6" in the neighbourhood of S.30,d. The work was carried out under heavy shell fire.	

WAR DIARY
or
INTELLIGENCE SUMMARY.
(Erase heading not required.)

Army Form C. 2118.

Place	Date	Hour	Summary of Events and Information	Remarks and references to Appendices
F4, 6, 5, 2,	21/8/16	10 AM	The battalion marched out of Camp and arrived at MORLANCOURT by 1 P.M.	
MORLANCOURT	22/8/16	10 AM	All transport including bicycles left by route march for HEUZECOURT, the battalion less transport remained in camp till next morning.	
MORLANCOURT	23/8/16	11:15 AM	The battalion left camp to entrain at MÉRICOURT. The train which was due to leave at 2 P.M. departed at 3.15 P.M.	
		9.15 P.M.	The battalion detrained at FIENVILLERS = CANDAS.	
HEUZECOURT	24/8/16	2 AM	The battalion arrived at HEUZECOURT and billeted for the day and night. Transports had arrived at 5 P.M. on 23rd Aug.	
HEUZECOURT	25/8/16	9 AM	The battalion marched out of billets and arrived at FROHEN-LE-GRAND at 11.30 AM. Billets accommodation for men was poor.	
FROHEN LE GRAND		4 P.M.	Orders were received that the battalion would continue march the following day.	
FROHEN LE GRAND	26/8/16	10 AM	The battalion marched out of billets and reached BOUBERS-SUR-CANCHE at 1 P.M. where the men halted for dinners.	
BOUBERS SUR CANCHE		2.15 P.M.	The battalion continued its march for FLAMINIEAMONT.	

Army Form C. 2118.

WAR DIARY
or
INTELLIGENCE SUMMARY.
(Erase heading not required.)

Place	Date	Hour	Summary of Events and Information	Remarks and references to Appendices
FLAMMERMONT	25/8/16	6 P.M.	The Battalion reached FLAMMERMONT at 4 P.M. and were in Billets by 5 P.M. Orders were received for Battalion to march next day as far as MONCHY CAYEUX.	
MONCHY CAYEUX	27/8/16	9 P.M.	The Battalion left FLAMMERMONT at 10 A.M. and halted 1 mile South west of WAVRANS for dinner. The Battalion continued at 2:15 P.M. and reached MONCHY CAYEUX at 3:15 P.M. Billets for the men were very scattered, and there was very little accommodation for officers. Orders were received at 4 P.M. for the Battalion to march next day to MAREST. ~~...~~	
MAREST	28/8/16	5 P.M.	The Battalion marched off from MONCHY CAYEUX at 8 A.M. and arrived at MAREST at 12:15 P.M. and were in Billets by 1 P.M.	
HOUCHIN	29/8/16	6 P.M.	The Battalion marched out of MAREST at 10 A.M. and reached HOUCHIN at 4:15 P.M. All ranks were settled in billets & huts by 6:0 P.M.	

Army Form C. 2118.

WAR DIARY
or
INTELLIGENCE SUMMARY.
(Erase heading not required.)

Instructions regarding War Diaries and Intelligence Summaries are contained in F. S. Regs., Part II. and the Staff Manual respectively. Title pages will be prepared in manuscript.

Place	Date	Hour	Summary of Events and Information	Remarks and references to Appendices
HOUCHIN	30/8/16	6.PM	The battalion remained in HOUCHIN all day and billeted for the night. Owing to heavy rain, permission was obtained to do the instead of proceeding to PHILOSOPHE.	
PHILOSOPHE	31/8/16	6.PM	The Battalion marched out of HOUCHIN at 12 Noon and arrived PHILOSOPHE at 5 PM. The C.O. reconnoitred the trenches in the Divisional front with the C.O.'s during the morning and the 3 Company Commanders during the evening (we relieve the 8/Lincoln ~~Bts.~~)	
~~PHILOSOPHE~~				

Eric Anson
Capt.
Capt. 20/K.R.R.C.

T2134. Wt. W708—776. 500000. 4/15. Sir J. C. & S.

Confidential.

War Diary
of
20th Bn. KINGS ROYAL RIFLE CORPS, (B.E.L. PIONEERS)

Vol 6.

From — 1st September 1916.   To — 30th September 1916.

Volume VI.

WAR DIARY
or
INTELLIGENCE SUMMARY.

Army Form C. 2118.

Place	Date	Hour	Summary of Events and Information	Remarks and references to Appendices
PHILOSOPHE	1/9/16	6 P.M.	The Battalion remained in PHILOSOPHE all day. Officers visited the working areas preparatory to getting their working parties detailed for the different duties.	
PHILOSOPHE	2/9/16	6 P.M.	Orders were received for working parties to be detailed for duty with 56th Field Company R.E. (the Cheshire Field Company) and the 253rd Tunnelling Company. Two officers were also detailed to supervise construction of tramways and the organisation of traffic. Two Companies (C & D) moved from PHILOSOPHE and billeted in MAZINGARBE. There two were ordered to supply 180 men each for work on duty only with the 56th F.de.R.E. A Company was detailed with 253rd T.C. to work on listening shafts Nos. 35, 36, 37, 38 & 40. The party to number 20, including 20 miners, 20 from the 26th KRR and 20 drawn from various Battalions.	
MAZINGARBE	3/9/16	6 P.M.	Headquarters removed from PHILOSOPHE to MAZINGARBE at 12 hours. A + B Companies remained in billets at ~~MAZINGARBE~~ PHILOSOPHE.	

WAR DIARY
or
INTELLIGENCE SUMMARY
(Erase heading not required.)

Army Form C. 2118.

Place	Date	Hour	Summary of Events and Information	Remarks and references to Appendices
MAZINGARBE	3/9/16	6 P.M.	B Company were ordered to detail 48 men to work on Trench mortar emplacements for the Cheshire F.C.R.E., in reliefs of 12 every six hours. The work consists of 4 emplacements, 2 in VERDUN ALLEY 1 in ESSEX LANE and 1 in HOLLY LANE, all to being just behind the support line on the above C.T's.	
		9 P.M.	The first relief of 12 men left PHILOSOPHE for work on T.M. emplacements, 2nd Lt BIDENCOPE in charge.	
MAZINGARBE	4/9/16	8 A.M.	The first relief of A Company under 2nd Lt THOMAS left for work on listening shaft with Captain BANKS. The relief consisted of 40 men and 18 miners. The first party for work at Dug out with 575 F.C. R.E. left at 9 a.m. 3/9/16 and worked till 9 P.m. 4/9/16 on constructing shelters for men. selves at CRUCIFIX DUMP near LOOS. Captain NEWMAN & Lt PENNA were in charge.	
		11 P.M.	The first relief of A Company worked from 10 A.m to 10 P.m on L.G's. L.G. H.Q. Timber was taken out, & northern lateral gallery was started 4'-	

WAR DIARY
INTELLIGENCE SUMMARY

Army Form C. 2118.

254th Bn. KING'S (LIVERPOOL) WAR CORPS. (B.E.F. FRANCE)

Place	Date	Hour	Summary of Events and Information	Remarks and references to Appendices
MAZINGARBE	4/9/16	11 P.m.	L.9.38 Southern lateral gallery extended 3ft. Northern was started. L.9.37 Finished taken out & cutting made 4 ft. The same work also done in L.9.36. 2 ft. lateral gallery cut in L.9.35. L.9.s 38, 37, 36, & 35 were blocked up with full sandbags. These were removed & used on front line trench. The men were unable to work long in L.9.35 owing to bad atmosphere. The reliefs of B Company carried on with T.M. emplacements under 2nd Lt. SEEMES and LANGRIDGE, taking over at 3 A.m. 9 A.m. 3 P.m. and 9 P.m.	
MAZINGARBE	5/9/16	11 P.m.	C Company took on work for 255 Field Coy R.E. at 10 A.m. upon the following Dug Outs in RESERVE LINE Nº 41 A, 42, 12, 47, 13 and 14. 2 officers (2nd Lts WILLIAMS & 2nd Lt TURBERVILLE) and 106 NCO's & men were to be responsible for work in an 8 hour shifts. A Company from 10 P.m. 4/9/16 to 10 A.m. 5/9/16 extended Northern lateral gallery at L.9.40 to 3ft. & cleared forecourt of debris. At L.9.38. They extended work 4ft & removed all full bags. At L.9.37 They extended work 3ft & removed debris, and at L.9.36, an extension of 2ft was done. Filled sandbags were used to build up work done in C.T.s & front line. work on L.9.37 ceased at 6 A.m. though bad atmosphere, no work from [?] in L.9. 35	

Army Form C. 2118.

WAR DIARY
or
INTELLIGENCE SUMMARY

(Erase heading not required.)

254th Bn. KINGS ROYAL RIFLE CORPS (B.E.F.)

Instructions regarding War Diaries and Intelligence Summaries are contained in F.S. Regs., Part II. and the Staff Manual respectively. Title pages will be prepared in manuscript.

Place	Date	Hour	Summary of Events and Information	Remarks and references to Appendices
MAZINGARBE	5/9/16	11 P.M.	B Company continued on 4 T.M. Emplacements at VENDIN ALLEY, ESSEX LANE & MAROC LANE with the usual shifts. A Company moved from PHILOSOPHE to MAZINGARBE for billets. 22 N.C.O's & men reported to 2/Lt VAN NESS at FOSSE 3 for work at tramway & dump at midday. 2nd Lts PARRY & GABEL also reported to 2/Lt VAN NESS. From 10 A.M. to 10 P.M. A Company cleared out all the galleries in L.9.s 40, 38, 37, + 36 and fixed in a set of timbers in each, and started cutting through the parados near the galleries to form dumps for filled sandbags. This work was held up for want of suitable timber.	
MAZINGARBE	6/9/16	10 A.M.	B Coy started on 4/9/16 to make Dug Outs in front line with East Riding R.E. 48 NCOs & men being employed in 4 shifts of 6 hours each. These shifts continued on work day & night. 2nd Lts ROUGHAN + SELNES superintended work in turn with other B Coy. officers. A Coy from 10 P.M. 5/9/16 to 10 P.M. 6/9/16 extended 4 fts timbered L.9.s 38 + 36 and extended 5 fts timbered in L.9.40. Cuttings through parados were continued, the one behind L.9.37 being almost completed. Work was impossible in L.9. 37 + 35 owing to bad atmosphere. 2nd Lts CHAMBERS + JONES + 2nd Lt SMITH take charge of shifts in turn with 2nd/Lt THOMAS under	
		11 P.M.	Capt BANKS. [From 6 A.M. to 10 P.M. 6/9/16. L.9.s 40, 38, 36 were extended 4 ft each about 4½ filled sandbags were removed and L.9.37 extended about 2 ft. 5 cuttings in parados continued]	

Army Form C. 2118.

WAR DIARY
or
INTELLIGENCE SUMMARY.
(Erase heading not required.)

Instructions regarding War Diaries and Intelligence Summaries are contained in F. S. Regs., Part II. and the Staff Manual respectively. Title pages will be prepared in manuscript.

Place	Date	Hour	Summary of Events and Information	Remarks and references to Appendices
MAZINGARBE	6/9/16	11 P.M.	No work on L.9.35 could be done owing to bad atmosphere. Work was continued by B. Coy on the 4 T.M. emplacements.	
MAZINGARBE	7/9/16	2 P.M.	C. Coy. from 10 a.m. 5/9/16 to 10 a.m. 7/9/16 did following work on Dug Outs with 5th Batt Coy. R.E. 41A started 2 entrances: 42, continued on entrance shafts: 12, completed entrance shafts: 47, existing Dug Out enlarged: 13, entrances worked on, and debris removed from 14. Owing to great fall of chalk in the dugout, work was abandoned & 146 substituted for work. 2nd Lieut. 3rd A.R. TURBERVILLE supervised the shifts of Eight hours each.	
		11 P.M.	A Coy from 10 P.M. 6/9/16 to 10 P.M. 7/9/16 continued lengthening L.9.s 40, 36, 37, 36, 35. About 7ft 6/10 ft. was cut in each L.G. except No. 35 only 5ft. having been done, owing to foul air. The 5 cuttings in parados were continued. B. Coy continued work on TM emplacements with the Cheshire F.T.M. R.E. and on dug out 5 in front line with East Riding R.E.	
MAZINGARBE	8/9/16	11 P.M.	A. Coy. from 10 P.M. 7/9/15 to 10 P.M. 8/9/16 extended L.9s 40, 36 & 36 by about 4 ft. work in L.9.s 37 & 35 not being possible owing to foul air. Firing to am & 7.10 P.M. They extended work in all cross laterals except L.9.36 about 3 ft. No firm lateral in L.9.37 was started. Timber was found not to be suitable. B. Company continued	

WAR DIARY or INTELLIGENCE SUMMARY

Army Form C. 2118.

16th Bn. Kings Royal Rifle Corps. (B.E.F)

Place	Date	Hour	Summary of Events and Information	Remarks and references to Appendices
MAZINGARBE	8/9/16	11 P.m.	Work on T.M. emplacements in VENDIN ALLEY, ESSEX LANE & HOLLY LANE and connected with dug outs in front line.	
MAZINGARBE	9/9/16	11 P.m.	A Coy from 10 P.m. 8/9/16 to 10 A.m. 9/9/16 lengthened Northern laterals an average 3 ft in L.9.3 40, 3.37, 9.36. There was no work on L.9.35, + only 1 pump was available, from 10 A.m. to 10 P.m. they continued lengthening at all L.9.s. Fixing 1 set of timber in 3 of them. D Coy from 10 P.m. 7/9/16 to 10 A.m. 9/9/16 carried on with building dug-outs Nos. M.581. Field Co. RE in 8 hr shift. C. Lt. WALLACE & Capt. NEWMAN supervised the work. The Coy was then relieved by C Coy. B Coy continued work on T.M. emplacements doing similar work to A Coy's. Billets were improved in front line.	
MAZINGARBE	10/9/16	11 P.m.	4. Coy from 10 P.m. 9/9/16 to 10 A.m. 10/9/16 lengthened N lateral work's Yd at L.9.40, removed defective timber & refitted one set at L.9.38 N lateral was lengthened 3ft 6 & all debris were removed. Northern lateral was lengthened 4ft at L.9.37. Similar work being done at L.9.36. No work was done on L.9.35. From 10 a.m. to 10 P.m. 1 set of timber was fixed at L.9.40. at L.9.38 the lateral was lengthened 3ft 6, 1 set of timber was fixed. Similar progress was accomplished at L.9.s 37, 36, + 35. Air pump was used at L.9.37. B Company continued making T.M. Emplacements and dug outs as hitherto.	

WAR DIARY or INTELLIGENCE SUMMARY

Army Form C. 2118.

Place	Date	Hour	Summary of Events and Information	Remarks and references to Appendices
MAZINGARBE	1/9/16	11 P.M.	A Coy. from 10 P.M. 10/9/16 to 10 A.M. 11/9/16 lengthened or deepened L.9.40 N to 20.48 + L.9.38 N to 12.35 - L.9.39 N to 10.48 and L.9.36 N to 15.42 7m. The dumps were all cleared & the trenches leading to them deepened. From 10 a.m. to 10 P.M. the lengthened L.9.5. 40 N 37 N 36 N & 35 N and two Bristol trenches. C. Coy from 10 A.M. 9/9/16 to 10 A.M. 11/9/16 were carried on with dug outs in Reserve Trenches with 56th Field Coy. in Northern sectors. No. 41 A shafts were completed & gallery commenced. B. No. 42 gallery started (29. 8" 12 worked gallery No. 47 continuation on enlargement. No. 13 Entrance completed & gallery started. No. 14 B entrances completed. They have relieved them by D Company. B Company continued making T.M. Emplacements and dug outs in Front Line.	
MAZINGARBE	12/9/16	11 P.M.	A Coy. from 10 P.M. 11/9/16 to 10 A.M. 12/9/16 made the following dugouts L.9.40 27t - 29, 38 31 65 L.9. 37 4ft - L.9. 36 3ft and L.9. 35 2ft + 3ft they worked on Pump Chambers & deepening the trenches to Dumps & cleared away all debris. From 10 P.M. to 10 P.M. the following was done. L.9.40 N 1st 15ft timber. L.9.38 S the same. L.9.38 N 4ft 6 1 ladder set-timbers L.9. 37 & 20t timbers. Pump Chambers were lengthened at L.9.35 & L.9 36 & one was started at 37. L.9.35 two inundible and work was greatly delayed by heavy working parties in the Front Line. B Coy. continued work on Dug Outs in Front Line,	

WAR DIARY or INTELLIGENCE SUMMARY

Army Form C. 2118.

Instructions regarding War Diaries and Intelligence Summaries are contained in F.S. Regs., Part II. and the Staff Manual respectively. Title pages will be prepared in manuscript.

(Erase heading not required.)

[Printed heading:] 2nd ROYAL IRISH CORPS. (B.E.F. PIONEERS)

Place	Date	Hour	Summary of Events and Information	Remarks and references to Appendices
MAZINGARBE	12/9/16	11 P.M.	and started fixing frames for gas projs in front line with Cheshire Regt. 2nd Lt. SELMES & Lt. ROUGHAN were in charge.	
" "	13/9/16	11 P.M.	A.Coy. from 10 P.M. 12/9/16 to 10 P.M. 13/9/16 made the following progress. L.G.40.N.3k - L.G.36n. 2F.6".-L.G.37n.4F.6½". -L.G.36n.1F.6".-L.G.35.N.1F.6½". They continued the boring at all L.G's & cleaned away all debris. 2 new pumps were obtained & frames in L.G's 35 & 36. From 10 a.m. to 10 P.M. they continued boring at L.G's 40.N, 36, 37, 36 & 35. average 3ft. Pumps worked continuously at L.G's 35, 36 & 37. D. Coy. from 10 a.m. 11/9/16 to 10 a.m. 13/9/16 worked on dug-outs in Reserve Trenches working with 35th Field Coy. Capt. NEWMAN & 2 Lt. WALLACE were in charge. B Coy continued fixing gas frames in front line and also making dug-outs in front line.	
" " " "	14/9/16	11 P.M.	A.Coy. from 10 P.M. 13/9/16 to 10 A.M. 14/9/16 continued boring by about Breeze 3F.6". L.G's 41, 38, 37, 36 & 35. Worked on T dumps & cleared away all debris. Pumps were working on 35, 36 & 37. From 10 A.M. to 10 P.M. progress continued in L.G's 4N 38", 37N 35 N. An average of 2 F.6" to 3 F.6". Tin boring was done throughout the working hours. Remainder of pumps at work on pump chambers & T dumps. The former are now complete for 35, 36 & 37. Work for 38 commenced. B Coy. continued making dug-outs in front line.	

Army Form C. 2118.

WAR DIARY
or
INTELLIGENCE SUMMARY.
(Erase heading not required.)

Instructions regarding War Diaries and Intelligence Summaries are contained in F. S. Regs., Part II. and the Staff Manual respectively. Title pages will be prepared in manuscript.

Place	Date	Hour	Summary of Events and Information	Remarks and references to Appendices
MAZINGARBE	15/9/16	11 P.M.	A Coy from 10 P.m. 14/9/16 to 6 A.m. 15/9/16 made the following progress. L.G.s 40 N Duplicated from 29'ft to 32 ft 6". 38 N from 25 ½ ft to 38 ft. 6": 37 N from 28 ft 6" to 32 ft 6". 36 N from 23 ft 6" to 25 ft. and 35 S from 6 ft to 4 ft. Work continued on all T dumps. Pumps working on 36, 35 and 37. From 10 A.m. to 7 P.m. L.G.s 40 N 38 N 37 N 36 N were Cup(?) down about 3 ft 6". Entrances were down in each. Work on H.Q. new dugout and Haming Drain 4th shaft another 8 ft. L.G. 35 was lightened 4 ft. Pumps were cleaned away and one fire bay finished. (was flown in) 2 ells was sunk to new order of Tunnel Pattern. C Company from 10 A.m. 13/9/16 to 10 A.m. 15/9/16 working on LMY.s 5 in Reserve Trenches Tn. 41 & 42. Work was carried out on Shelters. Shelters were completed at 12 & 13. The entrances were excel.(?) to work at POTEN ALLEY DUGOUTS & SQUAD WIRE DUGOUTS. The chalk in 41 & 42 A was estimated hard to making (Pigeon Stone). B Company continues making dug outs in front line and working on T.M. Emplacements.	
" "	16/9/16	11 P.M.	A Coy from 10 P.m. 15/9/16 to 10 A.m. 16/9/16 Completed L.G. 35 from 3 ft 6" to 37. L.G. 36 3 ft 6" to L.G. 35 3 ft 6" worked on all the drivings and Chambers. Pumps were at work on L.G.s 35, 36 & 37. No work was done on L.G. 40 by R.E. stores. B Coy continued making dug outs in front line and T.M. Emplacements.	

Army Form C. 2118.

26th Bn. KING'S ROYAL RIFLE CORPS, (B.E.F. PIONEERS)

WAR DIARY
or
INTELLIGENCE SUMMARY.
(Erase heading not required.)

Place	Date	Hour	Summary of Events and Information	Remarks and references to Appendices
MAZINGARBE	14/9/16	11 P.M.	From 10 A.m. to 10 P.m. A Coy carried out the following work L.9.38 & 39ft 1st number 38s & Front & forward gallery, 37n continued at 6ft 36in was lengthened 11ft and 35s 38ft. Timbering was put in and then sand pumps worked north in 35, 38 & 39. Spare men were now in carrying timber from dumps for extra work in listening sets. B Coy continued making dug outs in front line with the usual shifts of 12 men of the 6/K.R.R. and carried on with T.M. emplacements, men were also engaged on infantry D.O.K.	
NAZINGARBE	17/9/16	11 P.M.	A Coy from 10 P.m. 16/9/16 to 10 A.m. 17/9/16 lengthened L.9.38 from 33ft 6in to 37ft L.9.37 from 37ft 6in to 42ft 36 from 32ft 6 35ft = 35s from 6ft 6 to 11ft. Forward galleries in L.9.35 were started, & work continued on timber dumps, all others were clearing away. From 10 a.m. to 10 P.m. L.9s 38, 37, 36, & 35 were lengthened and timber fixed in all. The southern forward gallery of No 35 was started 4 cut to 3ft 6in. Sumps were sunk on 35, 36, & 37. D Coy from 16/9/16 10 P.m. to 17/9/16 10 A.m. continued as usual with dug outs by 69th hour shift to assist 25th Field Coy. E Nation & D Coy continued making dug outs in front line and T.M. Batteries were in charge. B Coy.	

Such casualties VERDIN ALLEY ESSEX LANE TOLLY LANE.

WAR DIARY / INTELLIGENCE SUMMARY

Army Form C. 2118.

18th Bn. KING'S ROYAL RIFLE CORPS, (B.E.F. FRANCE)

Place	Date	Hour	Summary of Events and Information	Remarks and references to Appendices
MAZINGARBE	17/9/16	11 P.M.	A Coy from 10 P.M. 17/9/16 to 11 A.M. 18/9/16. Casualties 1 O.R. Pte. 27 B. Coy (at hospital). Left half 6.9.36 to 6.9.37 - Right half 35 to 38 tip. 6.8 (worked) 27 ft to pump up to L.9.44 6.5. L.9.37 from 44ft 6½ to 46ft 6 to L.9.36 from 38 6½ to 40ft. The Southern Transom gallery L.9.35 was extended to 148 9 in. The Coy worked one bay 3 lengths & cleared away at Listening Pumps worked at L.9's 35, 36, 37. From 10 am to 10 P.M. The forward gallery L.9.38S was started - Left 2ft 1 Sect Timber replaced. L.9.37N was lengthened from 46ft 6 to 48ft 6 and 36N was lengthened from 3ft to 4ft in L.9.35 Northward gallery was advanced 4ft and all debris was cleared. The removal of sandbags impeded by French Instructions has ceased & workmen continued making improvements to Tunnel Line and T.M. dugs. Weather fair.	
MAZINGARBE	18/9/16	11 P.M.	A Coy from 10 P.M. 18/9/16 to 11 A.M. 19/9/16. Relieved by Mess. L.9.38N from 4ft 6 to 4ft 9. Bar. The Southern transom gallery from 9ft to 5ft L.9.37N was lengthened from 48ft to 49ft, 36v from 4ft to 4ft 2 b. No. 6 2 sets finishing in Northern Transom & relieved. L.9.35 Northern gallery was lengthened from 6ft to 7ft. 6ft Defensive Timber was ordered & replaced. Number of cartridges from 4 O.R.L. M.E.R.R L.9.38. In Rear transom gallery Set to 7ft 6 x 3ft 6 of R.E. casing was fixed. L.9.37 from 35ft to 41ft 6	

WAR DIARY or INTELLIGENCE SUMMARY

Army Form C. 2118.

30th Bn. KINGS ROYAL RIFLE CORPS, (B.E.L. PIONEERS)

Place	Date	Hour	Summary of Events and Information	Remarks and references to Appendices
MAZINGARBE	17/9/16	11 P.m.	L9.36.d war lengthened from 42ft 6ins to 45ft 6ins. The northern front gallery of L9.35 was lengthened from 11ft to 13ft. The southern ground gallery was started 2ft long. 3 Fire Bays were dug out & built up by orders of G.O.C. 9th Brigade. B Coy continued making dug outs in Front Line with usual shifts. The emplacements continued up till noon — morning working parties for the emplacements were then put onto From 10 A.m. 17/9/16 to 10 A.m. 17/9/16 C Coy carried on with the dug outs. The entrance to Signal dug out in POSEN ALLEY were completed while the entrance to Signal dug out in RAILWAY ALLEY signal dug out — were continued with. N. 41 & 13th galleries were completed & the 2nd one started. Work was done on 2nd gallery at N 42.d dug-out, while at N. 12 & 13 the 2nd galleries were completed (search was commenced on the 3rd gallery. Subaltern at N.14 were worked on. During heavy rain the shelters occupied as rest billets in GUN TRENCH became uninhabitable so that the parties due for rest from 6 A.m. 18.9.16 to 2 a.m. 19.9.16 occupies dug outs at N. 12 & 13 & consequently no work was done in them for that shift. The parties worked instead on dug out N 14.d & cleared a fall of earth up parapet of RAILWAY ALLEY.	

WAR DIARY or INTELLIGENCE SUMMARY

Army Form C. 2118.

16th Bn. KING'S ROYAL RIFLE CORPS, (B.E.F. France)

Place	Date	Hour	Summary of Events and Information	Remarks and references to Appendices
MAZINGARBE	20/9/16	11 P.M.	During the day parties working for East Ridings and Cheshire Field Coys and 58th R.E. Coy were cancelled owing to orders being received for the 3rd Division to move into the area. An extra working party for the 253rd Field Coy R.E. had been detailed from B Coy numbering 85 men. The fourth were only able to make little headway in the trenches before Cuinchy Breastwork. A Coy continued work to Tee 253rd tunnelled Coy from 10 P.M. 19/9/16 to 6 A.M. 20/9/16. L.9.38 southern forward gallery was camouflet fired from 30ft to 5ft. L.9.26 eastern hard 45ft 6ins to 49ft 6ins. for him from 30ft to 5ft. L.9.37 Lg 37 L.9.5 northern forward gallery new bore was inspected by trial contention of lime and was found detailed to L.9.8, 37 & 37.35 worked 4 hours in respirator the tamping. From 4 A.M. to 10 P.M. when air was given & direction altered in L.9.38 cartoon fitting placing 3 set of R.E. Canary were put in. At L.9.37 L.46 m.g was cleared out and defective timber replaced an advance of 1ft was made in both ends. L.9.36 m was being holed up to 17th end of R.E. Canary. At L.9.35 the northern forward gallery was lengthened up to 17th end of R.E. Canary were fixed, and the pump chamber was completed on L.9.38.	

WAR DIARY
or
INTELLIGENCE SUMMARY

Army Form C. 2118.

24th Bn. KINGS ROYAL RIFLE CORPS. (B.E.L. PIONEERS)

Place	Date	Hour	Summary of Events and Information	Remarks and references to Appendices
MAZINGARBE	2/9/16	11 P.m.	B, C, and D Companies continued in [strength] the village all day clearing up etc. A Coy from 10pm 20/9/16 to 10pm 21/9/16 finished off incomplete trenching at 2.9.38 northern pillar being C.T. northern pillar & T.6.0: T.6.b: L.9.37 southern pillar was lengthened up to T.6.0 T.6.b and 36 N by 15.5 ft. 2.9.37 [northern] pillar was lengthened at 6 to 9 ft 6 in and northern [forward] was [lengthened from] fitted with fittings from 10 to 4 ft 6 6 ft. Set of RE Casing were fixed. Debris was also cleared away from 10 P.m. 2.9.38 northern forward area lengthened at 6.9.37 & new lengthened up to 6.68 ft. L.9.36 or 6.55 ft and L.9.35 in [thous] up to 6.22 ft 65 debris was cleared away and T bump of [break] out.	
MAZINGARBE	21/9/16	6 P.m.	The last shift from A Coy returned about 4 after midday. From 10 P.m. 21/9/16 to 6 A.m. 22/9/16 L.9.38 northern was lengthened up to 5 ft. the [northern] trench No 16 12 ft 3 in L.9.37 southern from 0 to 3 ft. L.9.36 southern up to 5.9. ft 6 in and L.9.35 southern forward [gallery] was closed in which [work] was also carried on at [depth] 1.35 & 36 7 ft yard [listening] dumping in daylight. The Companies spent the day in packing up wagons & clearing up	

J.W.

Army Form C. 2118.

WAR DIARY
or
INTELLIGENCE SUMMARY.
(Erase heading not required.)

Instructions regarding War Diaries and Intelligence Summaries are contained in F. S. Regs., Part II. and the Staff Manual respectively. Title pages will be prepared in manuscript.

Place	Date	Hour	Summary of Events and Information	Remarks and references to Appendices
MAZINGARBE	22/9/16	6 P.M.	Billets.	
" "	23/9/16	8.15 a.m.	The Battalion started to march away by platoons at five min. intervals.	
MINES			Where the Companies & Transport formed up for the days march	
BURBURE	23/9/16	6 P.M.	The Battalion and Transport reached BURBURE at 4 P.M. and were in billets by 5 P.M. Orders were received to move next day to ENGUINEGATTE independently, the Battalion having marched to BURBURE with the 76th Brigade. The billeting accommodation at BURBURE was exceptionally good.	
ENGUINEGATTE	24/9/16	6 P.M.	The Battalion having marched out of BURBURE at 8.45 a.m. reached ESTRÉ BLANCHE at 1 P.M. in time to clear the village before the 76th Brigade arrived to billet there. The officers and officers mail had dinner & fed horses etc. just beyond the village, and just as the battalion was ready to move on, a billeting officer who had been sent on ahead returned with the news that there was no accommodation for two Companies only. B & C Companies and Batt. Transport sure that of A + B Companies went on to rest in Billets by 7 P.M. Engineers were held at 3rd Division HQ through 76th Brigade, and after some time the A & D Companies marched on to the destination and (Gomenant) in the battle	

T2134. Wt. W708—776. 500000. 4/15. Sir J. C. & S.

Army Form C. 2118.

20th Bn. KINGS ROYAL RIFLE CORPS. (B.E.L. PIONEERS)

WAR DIARY
or
INTELLIGENCE SUMMARY.
(Erase heading not required.)

Instructions regarding War Diaries and Intelligence Summaries are contained in F. S. Regs., Part II. and the Staff Manual respectively. Title pages will be prepared in manuscript.

Place	Date	Hour	Summary of Events and Information	Remarks and references to Appendices
ENGUINEGATTE	24/9/16	6 P.M.	A staff officer of the 30 Division came & interviewed certain inhabitants with the result that information for 1 more Company was secured. It was agreed that the 4 Company should move in the following morning.	
ENGUINEGATTE	25/9/16 6 P.M.		The 4 Companies started training on lines laid down in a scheme for training in accordance with Divisional Orders. Only a portion of the training has to be re-arrangement of billets. A Coy were placed in barns from the front (Day) but up with sheets & bivouacs for a permanent camp and the Servants being issued on the village.	
ENGUINEGATTE	26/9/16 8 P.M.		The battalion did Physical drill & bayonet fighting in the early morning; platoon & squad drill, bombing & musketry were carried on during the remainder of the day.	
" "	27/9/16 8 P.M.		The battalion did physical training, bayonet-fighting, digging fire trenches, close order drill, musketry and marching along roads.	
" "	28/9/16 8 P.M.		The battalion did physical training, bayonet fighting, close order drill, musketry, bombing, marching on roads and digging C.T's.	
" "	29/9/16 10 P.M.		The battalion did physical training, bayonet fighting, close order drill, musketry	J.M.

Army Form C. 2118.

16th Bn. KING'S ROYAL RIFLE CORPS, (B.E.F. FORCES)

WAR DIARY
or
INTELLIGENCE SUMMARY.
(Erase heading not required.)

Place	Date	Hour	Summary of Events and Information	Remarks and references to Appendices
ENGUINEGATTE	29/9/16	10 P.M.	marching always counter sloping direction. The men rested during the afternoon and practical construction of C.T.'s and fire trenches from 6.30 & 9.30 P.M.	
"	30/9/16	6 P.M.	The Battalion did physical training & bayonet fighting close order drill and musketry. Extended order drill was also practised and the men practised wire entanglements. Operation Orders prepared from those of 3rd Division for a practice attack to be carried out on 3rd October. Three Companies A.C.D. one to each Brigade, detailed "consolidate his 'KEEPS' both, 'B' Coy to be held in reserve. — — The work of the Companies in the HULLUCH-LOOS sector at MAZINGARBE, was extremely useful, and the experience gained and making deep dug-outs added greatly to the all round value of the men from a Proficiency point of view. 'A' Coy with Capt Ian BANKS, Lt CHAMBERS & 2nd Lt THOMAS did extremely good work. — — The following awards have been received by Officers and men of the Battalion :— 31.8.16 R.19674 Rfn A. WOOLSTON M.M.	

Army Form C. 2118.

20th Bn. KINGS ROYAL RIFLE CORPS. (B.E.L. PIONEERS)

WAR DIARY
or
INTELLIGENCE SUMMARY.
(Erase heading not required.)

Place	Date	Hour	Summary of Events and Information	Remarks and references to Appendices
ENGUINEGATTE	30/9/16			
	31.8.16		C.9857 Cpl. J. MARKS M.M.	
	" "		R.18752 Rfn C. STONE M.M.	
	11.9.16		Captain B.D. MELVILLE M.C.	
	" "		9126 C.S.M. E. PRATT D.C.M.	
	22.9.16		C.9305 Rfn G. FRESHWATER M.M.	
	" "		C.9167 Sgt. A. PHILLIPS M.M.	
	" "		Capt. & Adjt. J. JENKINS M.C.	

Lt. Col. Cdg.
20th (S) Batt. K.R.R.C. (B.E.L. Pioneers)

War Diary

20th (S) Battalion K.R.R. Corps (Pioneers)

1st to 31st October 1916

WAR DIARY
or
INTELLIGENCE SUMMARY. 13th Bn. KINGS ROYAL RIFLE CORPS, (B.E.L. PIONEERS)
(Erase heading not required.)

Army Form C. 2118.

Place	Date	Hour	Summary of Events and Information	Remarks and references to Appendices
ENGUINEGATTE	1/10/16	6.P.m	A conference was held by General G.O.C. 3rd Division at 3 P.m. on the night of the commencement of the attack which is to be carried out on Tuesday 3rd inst in connection with the training of the Division.	
"	2/10/16	8 P.m	In accordance with arrangements made at the conference by the G.O.C. the scheme of attack was practised during the morning by Battalions and by Brigades during the afternoon. Three Companies, A, C, & D having been allotted to 8th Brigade 9th Brigade and 76th Brigade respectively reported to the Brigade H.Q.rs at 1.30 P.m. Rain & wet weather the companies went ordered to return to camp.	
"	3/10/16	8 P.m	Divisional Operation were postponed until 4th inst- own to heavy rain. The companies dusk moved off but returned on arrival to Camps and stood too for the remainder of the night again.	
"	4/10/16	8 P.m	The Divisional Operations took place during wet weather. Operation commenced at 11 A.M. A, C, & D Companies marched to the rendez-vous	

WAR DIARY or INTELLIGENCE SUMMARY

Army Form C. 2118.

2/5th Bn. KING'S ROYAL RIFLE CORPS (B.E.F.)

Place	Date	Hour	Summary of Events and Information	Remarks and references to Appendices
ENGUINEGATTE	4/10/16	8 P.M.	of the 9th and 76th Brigades; but they did no work on consolidation of 'Keeps' as allotted in the scheme of operation. Each coy. had been made responsible for 2 'Keeps', which were to have been consolidated after the final objective had been reached. The companies were ordered to stand by until a trench-mortar demonstration had taken place, after which they returned to camp.	
MONCHY & CAYEUX	5/10/16	8 P.M.	A.M. The Battalion and all transport marched out from ENGUINEGATTE at 9.30 A.M. The men had dinner at PELFART at 1 P.M. The Battalion was billeted half an hour occasion more to being held up by Divisional Transport. After leaving PELFART, the Battalion had a clear road and reached MONCHY CAYEUX at 5.30 P.M., all ranks were in billets by 7 P.M.	
"	6/10/16	12 noon	The transport left at 6.30 to-day in order to reach OMEICOURT (Transport rendezvous) by 8 am. It then proceeded on to EYREE MANIN according to orders received regarding the move. Four officers & 150 other ranks left in motor buses at 9 A.M. for ACHEUX on receipt of orders from 1st Corps H.Q. They had to report to DAA & QMG at V6 Corps H.Q. at 10.30 A.M.	

Army Form C. 2118.

WAR DIARY
or
INTELLIGENCE SUMMARY

(Erase heading not required.)

20th Bn. KINGS ROYAL RIFLE CORPS, (B.E.L. PIONEERS)

Instructions regarding War Diaries and Intelligence Summaries are contained in F.S. Regs., Part II. and the Staff Manual respectively. Title Pages will be prepared in manuscript.

Place	Date	Hour	Summary of Events and Information	Remarks and references to Appendices
MONCHY CAYEUX	6/10/16	12 noon	The following officers left with the party:- Capt. J.C. BANKS, Lt. W.W. VAN NESS, 2nd Lt. THOMAS and 2nd Lt. SMITH. The remainder of the Battalion remained for the day and night in MONCHY CAYEUX.	
		5.30 P.M.	Orders were received from the 32nd Division with reference to entraining. Billeting party under 2nd Lt. BATEMAN was ordered to leave St POL Station at 1.55 A.M. on 7/10/16, and remainder of unit to leave that station by 10.55 P.M. train for ACHEUX.	
St POL	7/10/16	10.30 P.M.	The billeting party left as per orders, and the Battalion less 'C' Company & transports marched out of MONCHY CAYEUX at 7.45 P.M. reaching St POL Station at 9.30 P.M. Here news was received that train would not leave till 7 P.M. next day (8/10/16) so the men were placed in station shelter for the night 7/8 and the officers spent the night at the officers' club. The Battalion left St POL at 7.15 A.M. 8/10/16 and reached ACHEUX at 8.15 P.M. when they detrained and waited on road-side for orders; none having been received up to that time as to where the battalion was to billet that night. The billeting officer had arranged billets at PUCHEVILLERS, but the transport had received orders to move on to BEAUSSART. On its way through ACHEUX, the Cookers were dropped, and a meal was given to the men while orders were awaited. A dry ration had been drawn at St POL before departure that morning, but beyond this the men had nothing. At 10.20 P.M. orders were received for the Battalion to encamp with the D.C.L.I. Pioneers at BEAUSSART, so they moved off but on reaching BEAUSSART	
BEAUSSART	9/10/16	12 noon	It was found necessary to sleep in the open, there being no accommodation at all. All ranks were settled down by 11.30 A.M. 9/10/16. The billeting officer and party were conveyed by lorries from PUCHEVILLERS together with mens blankets which had been left there overnight for the unit. They reached BEAUSSART at 11.15 A.M.	

2449 Wt. W14957/Mgo 750,000 1/16 J.B.C. & A. Forms/C.2118/12.

WAR DIARY or INTELLIGENCE SUMMARY

Army Form C. 2118.

Place	Date	Hour	Summary of Events and Information	Remarks and references to Appendices
BEAUSSART	9/10/16	12 noon	'A' Company arrived at BEAUSSART Camp at 11.45 a.m. from BERTRANCOURT where they had billeted for the night 8/9. Previous to this the Company had been engaged on test-kitchen at LEALVILLERS and ACHEUX. All other Companies bivouacked for night 9/10 at BEAUSSART Camp, bivouacs having been obtained from 3rd Division.	
MAILLY MAILLET	9/10/16	6 P.M.	Battalion H.Q. removed from BEAUSSART Camp to quarters in MAILLY MAILLET. The C.R.E. issued following orders with regard to Companies' work in the new line:— 1 Coy. allotted to 515 Field Coy. R.E. as follows: ½ Coy. for Div. R.E. Dump, BEAUSSART, 1 platoon for Dum't Reserve B'de dugouts, 1 platoon for Tramways. This work was given to 'D' Coy. 1½ Coys. to work under orders of O.C. EAST RIDING Field Coy. R.E. on dugouts in Northern Sector: this work was given to 'A' Coy. and ½ of 'B' Coy. — 1½ Coys. to work under orders of O.C. CHESHIRE FIELD Coy. R.E. on B'de dugouts for Southern Brigade in the Southern area: this work was allotted to 'C' Coy. and ½ of 'B' Coy.	
MAILLY MAILLET	10/10/16	11 P.M.	'A' 'B' and 'C' Coys moved from BEAUSSART Camp to billets in MAILLY MAILLET. 'D' Coy took over huts in BEAUSSART Camp from D.C.L.I. Pioneers, that unit having moved out of the area during the morning. Lt. W.W. VAN NESS and 50 men went to COLINCAMPS to take over Divisional Bombing Stores and billeted there until further orders. 'C' Coy from 9 P.M. 9 Oct to 9 P.M. 10 Oct worked in 4 shifts of 6 hours each on B'de H.Q. dugouts under Sherwood R.E. Capt NEVILLE arranged shifts in charge of Lt. WILLIAMS, 2nd Lt. TURBERVILLE and 2nd Lt. GASSELL and 2nd Lt. PARRY. The following work done:— both faces advanced 3' 6" timbering 5.5 by	

WAR DIARY
or
INTELLIGENCE SUMMARY

Army Form C. 2118.

20th Bn. KING'S ROYAL RIFLE CORPS, C.E.L. PION...

Place	Date	Hour	Summary of Events and Information	Remarks and references to Appendices
MAILLY MAILLET	10/10/16	11 P.m.	South face — advanced 3' of timbering & 4 sets. East face — advanced 2' & timbering 3 sets. Maintenance with/out Major INGLIS arranged following work for 'D' Coy under 56th F.C. R.E. 2nd Lt LOCKWOOD + 38 men for Tramway to work nightly from 4.45 P.m. to 12.15 A.m. 2nd Lt PENNA and 2nd Lt BATEMAN + 40 men to work in reserve line in 6 hour shifts. Capt NEWMAN & 80 men on dugouts near Reserve daily on Div. R.E. Dumps from 8 A.m. to 5 P.m. Orders were detailed to work daily on Div. R.E. Dumps from 7 P.m. that transport would have to move further back from BEAUSSART next morning.	
MAILLY MAILLET	11/10/16	11 P.m.	On night 10/11 'B' Coy worked in three parties each composed of 1 officer + 40 N.C.O.s & men. 2nd Lt SELMES' party widened & deepened SACKVILLE AVENUE between RAILWAY AVENUE & SOUTHERN AVENUE. 2nd Lt ROUGHAN's party dug new trench from SOUTHERN AVENUE & SACKVILLE AVENUE and improved latter. 2nd Lt FEARBY's party worked on dugouts in ECZEMA TRENCH in future to be known as RAILWAY AVENUE. From 9 P.m. to 9 P.m. 115 'C' Coy worked on dug-outs in DUNMOW TRENCH for B.H.Q. as before in 4 shifts of 6 hours each. Dugout No 285 also continued with, an advance of 3'.6" was made in 'A' face, 4ft. in 'B' face, and 4 1/2' 6" in 'C' face. Timbering 5 sets in 'A' face, Timbering 7 sets in 'B' face and 5 sets of timber were placed in 'C' face. On 10th Oct. 'A' Coy supplied 1 officer + 60 N.C.O.s + men for work on Brigade Baths Q. Dug outs from 3.30 P.m. to 9.30 P.m. Another party of the same strength with Lieut Rideal R.E. R.E. from 3.30 P.m. to 9.30 P.m. and was relieved by another party from 9.30 A.m. on 11th Oct, on the same day worked on dugouts from 3.30 P.m. to 9.30 P.m. on the same day. Another party which worked from 9 to a field dose to ACHEUX in accordance with D'visional Orders received overnight. 'D' Coy worked as usual during night 10/11. The Transport moved during the day. The party for the tramway supplied & 'D' Coy worked as usual during night, and the two parties at work on dug-outs for Brigade H.Q. continued on as usual, and the two parties at work on dug-outs for Brigade H.Q. continued on as usual, and	

2449 Wt. W14937/M90 750,000 1/16 J.B.C. & A. Forms/C.2118/12.

WAR DIARY or INTELLIGENCE SUMMARY

Army Form C. 2118.

Place	Date	Hour	Summary of Events and Information	Remarks and references to Appendices
MAILLY MAILLET	11/10/16	11 P.M.	The party in charge of Div. R.E. Dump continued as arranged.	
" "	12/10/16	11 P.M.	On night 11/12 "B" Coy's parties worked as follows:- 1 Party under 2nd Lt. LANGRIDGE continued on Dugouts in ECZEMA AVENUE. 1 Party under 2nd Lt. SKELMES continued in Avenue deepening SACKVILLE AVENUE, another party under 2nd Lt. ROUGHAN continued digging and French from SOUTHERN AVENUE to SACKVILLE AVENUE and improved entry to fourth party carried on with Dugouts in ECZEMA TRENCH. "D" Coy carried on the work with the exception that MAJOR INGLIS took over dump from Capt. NEWMAN, who was appointed to take over temporary command of "C" Coy 13/10/16 vice Capt. MELVILLE who had to go to hospital for treatment. 2nd Lt. PENNA & 2nd Lt. BATEMAN continued to be in charge of the working parties during the night. L/Cpl. PENNA & 2nd Lt. BATEMAN continued in charge of night. NCO's & 3 knees. "A" Coy from 6.30 p.m. to 12.30 a.m. night 11/12 had 1 Officer & D.H.Q. platoons on work in C.T. 's with Sgt Riding E.E. R.E. from 3.30 a.m. to 9.30 a.m. work was continued on Dugouts. 1 N.C.O. and 12 men worked during the day on Dugouts. "C" Coy carried on with shifts from 9 p.m. to 7 a.m. & at 7 p.m. 12 in Dug-outs in DUNMOW trench & in B13 M.D.	
" "	13/10/16	11 P.M.	The following work was done by A Coy. 12-13 Oct. 1 Officer & 40 NCO's & men worked from 9 p.m. 6.3 a.m. in B13 & Dugouts with Sgt Riding R.E. 1 Officer & Sgt 17 & 4 platoons worked from 6.30 P.M. to 12.30 a.m. on repairing NORTHERN AVENUE carrying & fixing up trench boards then 1 Officer & 40 NCO's & men from 9 a.m. to 3 P.M. 13th Oct under Battn H.Q on Dugouts under East Ridings while a party of 1 NCO & 10 men worked on fixing up trench boards in NORTHERN AVENUE from 9.30 a.m. to 4 P.M. 13th "B" Coy worked night 12/13 as follows:- 1 Officer 12 Lt. LANGRIDGE & 40 N.C.O's & men continued with construction of Dugouts in ECZEMA avenue from 2 P.M. to 11 P.M. 1 Officer 12 Lt. DIGNEOPS Superintendent of NCBoots, & carrying & deepening SACKVILLE avenue & laying trench boards, & also then party of 40 N.C.O's & men	

WAR DIARY or INTELLIGENCE SUMMARY

Army Form C. 2118.

20th Bn. KINGS ROYAL RIFLE CORPS (B.E.F. PIONEERS)

Place	Date	Hour	Summary of Events and Information	Remarks and references to Appendices
MAILLY MAILLET	13/10/16	11 P.M.	Working on improvement of trench from SOUTHERN AVENUE & SACKVILLE AVENUE & also trench from 9 P.M. to 4 A.M. Another party of 40 N.C.O.'s been continued construction of dug outs in ECZEMA TRENCH. Capt. B.D. MELVILLE left for hospital during the morning. 'D' Coy. continued work on BEAUSART Dump and Dugouts for D.H.Q. and supervision of work upon Tramways.	
MAILLY MAILLET	14/10/16	11 P.M.	'A' Coy. supplied following working parties from 6.30 P.M. 13th to 12.30 A.M. 14th for deepening & digging drainage trench in NORTHERN AVENUE near EDEN TRENCH, 57 N.C.O.'s & men under 2/Lt THOMAS. — 2/Lt THOMAS & 40 N.C.O.'s & men worked between 2 P.M. & SELMES. — 'B' Coy. supplied following working parties; 40 H.Q. Dugouts from 9 P.M. to 3 A.M. 'B' Coy. with East-Ridings in charge of 2/Lt. LANGRIDGE & N.C.O.'s & men on construction of Dugouts, 2 Parties each of 40 N.C.O.'s & men under Lt. ECZEMA AVENUE from 2 P.M. to 11 P.M. — 2 Parties each of 40 N.C.O.'s placed Trench Boards M/LEWAN MONK trench & LEGEND drawing and placed Trench Boards ROUGHAN deepened & widened MONK trench & LEGEND drawing on a carrying party to in positions from 9 P.M. to 3 A.M. 184 + 15 men were sent as a carrying party to East Ridings in ECZEMA avenue. This party worked from 2 A.M. to 8 A.M. 2/Lt. E.D. BATEMAN left for hospital, 2/Lt PARRY taking over his work temporarily on D.H.Q. Dugouts with 6 & Field Coy. 'C' Coy from 9 P.M. 13th to 9 P.M. 14th worked in 4 shifts on Dug out No 285 in DUNMOW TRENCH. 16 shifts were at work during the night 12/13. The shifts of 40 men working under East Riding R.E. were reduced to 20 men, 60 men thus being released for working on improvement of trenches. 'D' Coy. continued work on BEAUSART DUMP, Dug outs for D.H.Q. & supervision of Tramways.	
MAILLY MAILLET	15/10/16	11 P.M.	'A' Coy from 9 A.M. to 3 P.M. 14/10/16 supplied 42 N.C.O's & men in charge East Riding Rifle Cos 2nd Lt SMITH was in charge. From 9.30 A.M. 6 4 P.M. 1 N.C.O. 12 men & trench boards in NORTHERN AVENUE. From 10 P.M. 14th to 3 A.M. 15th etc.	

WAR DIARY or INTELLIGENCE SUMMARY

Army Form C. 2118.

10th Bn. KING'S ROYAL RIFLE CORPS. (B.E.F. FRANCE)

Place	Date	Hour	Summary of Events and Information	Remarks and references to Appendices
MAILLY MAILLET	15/10/16	11 P.M.	1 Sgt. & 20 N.C.O's & men of "A" Coy worked on dug outs with Earl Ridge R.E. and Spr. with 10 P.M. to 3 a.m. 1st Off. "A" Coy supplied about 25 N.C.O.'s and men of 2nd. A. FEARBY on firing trench boards & drainage Ration & Dump PLS in NORTHERN AVENUE, from 9 a.m. to 3 P.M. 1 Sgt & 20 N.C.O.s & men continued work on dug outs with East RIDINGS R.E. and 2nd Lt THOMAS and 52 N.C.O's and men (A myson with L NORTHERN AVENUE C.T. between HITTITE trench and the SUCRERIE and SD from 9.30 P.M. to 3 a.m. "B" Coy supplied 2 parties of 40 N.C.O's men each on supporting NORTH trench and LEGEND trench from 7.30 P.M. to 11.30 a.m. 2 latrines with seats consisting of 2 N.C.O's & men worked on Dug outs in ECZEMA Avenue also from 2 P.m. to 11 a.m. The other from 2 P.M. to 11 P.M. Another party at the rear trench near ... with the Rifles with the rations CENTRAL avenue under 2nd Lt LANGRIDGE "C" Coy continued with the RAPL with strengthening R.E's in support No 295 in DUNMOW trench. The SKIS St & 20 men working with East Ridge R.E. were employed ... and also men and ... to trench improvement works as from night 15/6. "D" Coy continued on DIV. Dug outs and Experiments of Tunnery & BEAUSSART dump of 20 men from 4 P.m. to 10 P.m. 15th Oct. "A" Coy provided 5 off N.C.O's & men for work	
MAILLY MAILLET	16/10/16	11 P.M.	on NORTHERN avenue east of HITTITE trench ... sunny trench for to etc. Pte. LUX was impeded by shortage of material. 2nd Lt. SMITH was in charge. Conference with C.R.E. at 9.30 a.m. Following work notified & carried through the event of attack being carried through successfully 5 3rd & 2nd DUGOUTS. "B" & "C" Coys to consolidate SERRE "A" Coy & 3 platoons of "D" Coy to dig CT's from JOHN TUNNEL, MARY TUNNEL, ECZEMA TUNNEL & GABY TUNNEL to GERMAN FRONT LINE.	

WAR DIARY
or
INTELLIGENCE SUMMARY

Army Form C. 2118.

20th Bn. KINGS ROYAL RIFLE CORPS. (B.E.L. PIONEERS)

Place	Date	Hour	Summary of Events and Information	Remarks and references to Appendices
MAILLY MAILLET	16/10/16	11 P.M.	'A' Coy from 9.30 A.M. & 4 P.M. had 73 N.C.O's & men under 2½/Lt PERRY dp work on front trench boards; digging drains & forming place on NORTHERN AVENUE from SACKVILLE STREET. Another party 68 strong under 2½/Lt THOMAS continued work of similar character on NORTHERN AVENUE between HITTITE TRENCH and Obstrucksen in 2 tiers, wire removed, + 170m of boards wire fixed. 'B'Coy from 9.30 P.M. & 4.30 P.M. 4 th provided 2 parties of 40 N.C.O's + men each in widening & deepening LEGEND TRENCH and improving part of RAILWAY AVENUE & SOUTHERN AVENUE. L BIDENCOPE was in charge. Another party of 20 N.C.Os & men worked on improving RAILWAY AVENUE towards Front line and laying French trench boards from 2 A.M. to 11 P.M. Another party of 40 N.COs worked on improving CENTRAL AVENUE including travel fleurs, from 8.30 A.M. to 6.30 P.M. There worked an improved RAILWAY AVENUE started at 9 P.M. & worked until 11 P.M. a second relief for work on RAILWAY AVENUE started at 9 P.M. & worked until 11 P.M. 'C' Coy worked in 4 shifts of 6 hours each on Dugout N° 285 in DUNMOW TRENCH from 9 P.M. 15 E. to 9 P.M. 16 § incl.	
MAILLY MAILLET	17/10/16	11 P.M.	'A' Coy from 9.30 A.M. & 4 P.M. Suffield 78 N.C.O's + men under 2½/Lt SMITH on NORTHERN AVENUE chiefly between HITTITE + POLLAND trench; trench boards were fixed and the trench deepened & widened. Another party under 2½/Lt LANGRIDGE constituting 6-5 N.C.Os & men continued on same work from 4 P.M. to 8.45 P.M. 'C' Coy worked on N° 285 with 3 shifts of 6 hours each & 1 shift of 3 hours from 9 P.M. 16 to 6 P.M. 17. 'B' Coy supplied 2 parties of 40 N.C.o's + men each under 2/Lt SEAMES for widening & improving LEGEND TRENCH + laying trench boards from 11 P.M. 16 to 5 A.M. 17. 2 more parties each 20 strong worked on improvement of RAILWAY AVENUE from new OBSERVATION WOOD to Front line. From 2 A.M. to 7 A.M. & from 4 P.M. to 9 P.M.	

WAR DIARY
or
INTELLIGENCE SUMMARY

(Erase heading not required.)

Army Form C. 2118.

Place	Date	Hour	Summary of Events and Information	Remarks and references to Appendices
MAILLY MAILLET	17/10/16	11 P.M.	Another party of 40 NCOs & men carried on with improvements of CENTRAL AVENUE from 8:30 a.m. to 5:30 p.m. "D" Coy carried on with Dug-outs for Bn.H.Q. and work upon tramway & dumps.	
MAILLY MAILLET	18/10/16	11 P.M.	A fog. Sent a party of 78 N.C.O.s & men under 2nd Lt THOMAS to work from 9:30 a.m. to 4 p.m. the NORTHERN AVENUE as far as ROLAND TRENCH was completed in repairs. Another party of 17 Bty under 2nd Lt SMITH worked at cleaning out & draining NORTHERN AVENUE between MONK TRENCH & ROB ROY. from 4 P.M. to 10:15 P.M. 'C' Coy from 12 midnight 17/18 to 6 P.M. 18 continued work at Dug out of No D85 at DUNMOW TRENCH. "B" Coy supplied a party of 60 men from 7 to 11 P.M. 17 & 6 a.m. 18 on improving condition of SACKVILLE STREET under 2E ROUGHAN. Another party of 40 started work at 18 on improving CENTRAL AVENUE and cleaning away debris caused by shell fire from 8:30 a.m. to 5:30 p.m. "D" Coy continued work on Bn.H.Q. dug-outs, tramway and dumps.	
MAILLY MAILLET	19/10/16	11 P.M.	"B" Coy supplied 40 men from 6:30 a.m. to 5:30 p.m. on improving CENTRAL AVENUE. trench boards were fixed and the drainage of trench was mended. 2 parties of 40 men each were employed from 9:30 p.m. 18 to 6:0 A.M. 19 on digging C.T. from ROB ROY to front line in continuation of NORTHERN AVENUE under Lt. BIDENCOPE. Another party of 40 men worked from 7:30 P.M. 18 to 4:30 a.m. 19 on repairing damaged trench at junction of SACKVILLE STREET & RAILWAY AVENUE under 2nd Lt SELMES. Orders were received at 9:30 p.m. that the 3 companies & Head Quarters were to move from MAILLY MAILLET by 12 noon 20 Oct to neighbourhood of COLINCAMPS. So all working parties for night 19/20 were cancelled, with the exception of "D" Coy which carried on work as usual on Bn.H.Q dug-outs and tramway & dump.	
P.C. Central (Map. France 57D)	20/10/16	8 P.M.	The 3 companies & H.Q moved to camps alongside "D"Company at P.C. Central Map 12 noon. The afternoon was spent in settling cover for the men and working parties started again at 6 P.M. "B" Coy supplied 3 parties from 9:30 P.M. 19 to 4:30 A.M. 20 with 2 Ex men with Lt OAKLEY on repairing SOUTHERN AVENUE, RAILWAY AVENUE and HITTITE TRENCH. Parties carried	

WAR DIARY
or
INTELLIGENCE SUMMARY

Army Form C. 2118.

20th Bn. KINGS ROYAL RIFLE CORPS, (B.E.F. PION...)

(Erase heading not required.)

Place	Date	Hour	Summary of Events and Information	Remarks and references to Appendices
P.6. Central (Map France) (57 D)	2/4/16	8 P.M.	'B' Coy supplied another party from 9.30 a.m. to 5.30 P.M. on improving CENTRAL AVENUE and dugout. New trench boards. 'D' Coy continued work on D.H.Q dug outs and tramway & dumps.	
" "	21/10/16	11 P.M.	'A' Coy supplied a party of 51 men under 2/Lt THOMAS which worked from 9.30 a.m to 4 P.M. carrying up trench boards gurrats and continuing improvement of NORTHERN AVENUE between CAMPION TRENCH and ROB ROY TRENCH. Another party from the Coy 69 strong from 4 P.M. to 10 P.M. cleaned out and deepened about 200 yds. of NORTHERN AVENUE from ROB ROY trench towards the front line; trench boards were carried up and placed nearby for fixing. 'B' Coy supplied 3 parties with Cheshire F.C.R.E. from 9.30 P.M. to 3.30 A.M. night 20/21 repairing HITTITE TRENCH, SOUTHERN AVENUE & RAILWAY AVENUE. A fourth party was employed carrying material to forward dumps between ROB ROY & front line from 6 P.M. to 12 midnight.	

Army Form C. 2118.

WAR DIARY
or
INTELLIGENCE SUMMARY

16th Bn. KING'S ROYAL RIFLE CORPS (Church Lads Brigade)

(Erase heading not required.)

Instructions regarding War Diaries and Intelligence Summaries are contained in F. S. Regs., Part II. and the Staff Manual respectively. Title Pages will be prepared in manuscript.

Place	Date	Hour	Summary of Events and Information	Remarks and references to Appendices
Pt Central	23/10/16	10 p.m.	News was received during the day that Lt Col. E. Murray had been wounded in Southern Avenue about 5.30 pm. & immediately took over command (Major R Beigler). Three Companies A, B, & C were engaged on the upkeep of communication trenches and half of D Coy. on the repair and maintenance of existing railway from Euston Dump forward and half of D. Coy. on L.M.K. 3rd Div R. E. Dump.	
Pt Central	24/10/16	10 p.m.	The three Coys A, B, C. continued work on C.T's "Bluff Northern, Central, Southern Avenues." D. Coy. were again distributed half on Railway and Railway line and half on 3rd Div R E Dump.	
Pt Central	25/10/16	10 p.m.	The three Coys A. B. C. continued work on Northern, Central, Southern Avenues. B Coy had parties in trees in Durnamu, and Hittite. D. Coy. were distributed on the 23rd and 24th inst.	
Pt Central	26/10/16	10 p.m.	Three platoons of "A" Coy., 4 Platoons B. Coy., and 3 Platoons "D" C. Coy., were engaged on the upkeep of C.T's., 1 Platoon "A" Coy. and 1 Platoon "C" Coy. was engaged on the formation of forward dumps for use forward from Euston. D. Coy. were engaged while tracks from above distributed.	
Pt Central	27/10/16	10 p.m.	"A" Coy. 2 Platoons clearing Northern and Central and 1 Rob Roy. 2 Platoons clearing Northern and Central from Rob Roy to front line. "B" Coy. 4 Platoons on upkeep of C.T's and construction of Welsh Trench. "C" Coy. 2 Platoons clearing Railway Ave west of Rob Roy. 2 Platoons clearing Railway from Rob Roy to front line. "D" Coy. distributed as above.	CL

2449 Wt. W14957/M90 750,000 1/16 J.B.C. & A. Forms/C.2118/12.

Army Form C. 2118.

WAR DIARY
or
INTELLIGENCE SUMMARY
(Erase heading not required.)

20th Bn. KINGS ROYAL RIFLE CORPS. (B.E.L. PIONEERS)

Instructions regarding War Diaries and Intelligence Summaries are contained in F.S. Regs, Part II. and the Staff Manual respectively. Title Pages will be prepared in manuscript.

Place	Date	Hour	Summary of Events and Information	Remarks and references to Appendices
Pypyhyry 1916 Pt Central	28/10/16	10 p.m.	3 Coys A.B.C. were engaged on the upkeep of the following main C.T.s Northern, Central, Railway, and Southern Avenues. 'D' Coy was Plat. assisting the R.E.'s in constructing a light railway from Couneller to Euston, 1 Platoon on maintenance of existing railway, and 2 Platoons in 3rd Div. R.E. Dump.	
Couneller	29/10/16	12 n.n.	3 Coys A.B.C. were distributed as on the 28th inst. and 'D' Coy. were also distributed as on the 28th inst. 2½ Coys (A, D, and ½ C) and Head Quarters moved into billets at Couneller. The frontier left Pt Central at 10½ a.m. and the whole movement was completed by 11:30 p.m. 1½ Coys. (B + ½ C) remain in huts and bivouacs at Pt 6 central.	
Couneller	30/10/16	10 p.m.	'A' Coy and 2 Platoon 'C' Coy were engaged on the upkeep of Northern, Central, and Railway Avenues. 'B' Coy and 2 Platoons of 'C' Coy were engaged on work in Southern Av, Shuttle, and Josephine Trenches under the Cheshire Field Coy R.E. 'D' Coy were distributed as above.	
Couneller	31/10/16	10 p.m.	The above Coys A.B.C. continued their work on the maintenance of the above C.T.s. 'D' Coy were again distributed on railway work and carpentry work on the 3rd Div. R.E. Dump.	

R. Stylr. Lyn.
Comg. 20 L.K.R.R.C.

A/7815/A/23.

Officer i/c Adjutant General's Office
at the Base.

The attached War Diary of 20th Battalion K.R.R.C. (Pioneers) is forwarded in continuation of my A/7815/A/23 of 5th instant.

It is now understood that the Diary of 16th Divisional Supply Column mentioned in my letter of 5/11/16, was sent to you direct, and not through H.Q. Vth Corps as stated.

13/11/1916.

Major General,
Commanding 3rd Division.

A/7815/A/23.

Officer i/c Adjutant General's Office
  at the Base.

  The attached War Diary of 20th Battalion K.R.R.C. (Pioneers) is forwarded in continuation of my A/7815/A/23 of 5th instant.

  It is now understood that the Diary of 16th Divisional Supply Column mentioned in my letter of 5/11/16, was sent to you direct, and not through H.Q. Vth Corps as stated.

             Pragnell, Capt. for Major General,

13/11/1916.   Commanding 3rd Division.

WAR DIARY or **INTELLIGENCE SUMMARY**

Army Form C. 2118.

20th K.R.R.C. Vol 8

Place	Date	Hour	Summary of Events and Information	Remarks and references to Appendices
Courcelles	1/11/16	10 p.m.	3 Coys. A.B.C. were engaged on the upkeep of the following C.T's; Northern, Central, Railway, and Southern Avenues, Hibble, Summum and 15-teneur Trenches. "D" Coy. were distributed 2 Platoons on maintenance of light Railway and 2 Platoons on Carpentry at the 3rd Division R.E. Dump.	
Courcelles	2/11/16	10 p.m.	The three Companies A. B & C. continued the work on the above C.T's. "D" Coy. was redistributed as follows: 1½ Platoons on 3rd Division R.E. Dump. ½ Platoon on Light Railway. 2 Platoons on Trench Mortar Emplacements – Whole 56th Inft. Bde. T.E. 2nd Div. and continued	
Courcelles	3/11/16	10 p.m.	All four Companies were distributed as on the same work.	
Courcelles	4/11/16	10 p.m.	The four companies were again distributed as on 3/11/16 and carried on with the same work	
Courcelles	5/11/16	10 p.m.	Work was continued on the C.T's by A.B. & C Coys. "D" Coy. carried on with the R.E. Dump, the Light Railway, and the Trench Mortar Emplacements.	
Courcelles	6/11/16	10 p.m.	Work was carried on by A.B.C. Coys. on the above C.T's. 1 Platoon of "A" Coy. constructed a Ramp for Artillery just east of Pioneers & Colin camp. "D" Coy. carried on with the same work as on 5/11/16	of L

Army Form C. 2118.

WAR DIARY
or
INTELLIGENCE SUMMARY

(Erase heading not required.)

Instructions regarding War Diaries and Intelligence Summaries are contained in F. S. Regs., Part II. and the Staff Manual respectively. Title Pages will be prepared in manuscript.

Place	Date	Hour	Summary of Events and Information	Remarks and references to Appendices
Courcelles	7/11/16	10 p.m.	A.B.C. Coy carried on with work on C.T's. The one Platoon of "D" Coy finished the Ramp for Artillery. "D" Coy carried on with same work as on 6/11/16	
Courcelles	8/11/16	10 p.m.	A.B.C. Coys cleared the men C.T's; the new reinforcement one Platoon from A.B.C. Coys practiced rapid wiring all day. "D" Coy carried on with their usual work.	
Courcelles	9/11/16	10 p.m.	The whole of A.B.C. Coys practiced rapid wiring all morning. They marched off at 3:30 p.m. and started work on the wiring of the whole Divisional Front along Posh Roy at about 6:30 p.m. At 8:30 p.m. the work was all well in hand and very good progress was being made. "D" Coy carried on their usual work.	
Courcelles	10/11/16	10 p.m.	The three companies A.B.C. returned to Courcelles about 3 a.m. after completing their task. The whole of the Divisional Front was wired with 10 yd close wire and 90 yd apart, 30' in thickness. The companies rested during the day. "D" Coy carried on with their usual work.	
Courcelles	11/11/16	10 p.m.	A.B.C. Coys cleared the men C.T's. "D" Coy carried on with usual work.	
Courcelles	12/11/16	10 p.m.	The four companies spent the day completing preparations and organizations for forthcoming operations. I inspected all four companies during the afternoon and found all preparations were complete	P.L.

2449 Wt. W14957/M90 750,000 1/16 J.B.C. & A. Forms/C.2118/12.

WAR DIARY or INTELLIGENCE SUMMARY

Army Form C. 2118.

Place	Date	Hour	Summary of Events and Information	Remarks and references to Appendices
Courcelles	12/11/16	11.30 p.m.	The 1½ Coys (B and ½ C) moved from Pt Central to-night. 'B' Coy took up their position in Shittité Trench leaving Pt Central at 7 p.m. ½ C. Coy with baggage and details of 'B' Coy left Pt Central at 10 p.m. and moved into billets at Courcelles, move being completed by 11.30 p.m. 1 Platoon of 'D' Coy took up their position near Euston Dump to be in readiness for work on Light Railway.	
Courcelles	13/11/16	10 p.m.	A, C, and ½ D. Coy stood by all day ready to move at a moment's notice. At 8 p.m. orders were received from the C.R.E. for these Coys to be prepared to move at an hour's notice. 1 Platoon of 'D' kept the Light Railway in working order, whilst the other Platoon of 'D' continued work on the Dump. 'B' Coy returned to billets in Courcelles from Shittité Trench under orders of the Major-General Commanding 3rd Division, at 9 p.m.	
Courcelles	14/11/16	10.5 p.m.	The three companies A, B, + C were all employed on clearing up C.T.s. 'D' Coy had two platoons clearing Rob Roy, one platoon on the light Railway and one platoon on the 3rd Division R.E. Dumps. The platoon that had been living near the Light Railway returned to Courcelles about 12 m.n. with the exception of the small permanent guard.	
Courcelles	15/11/16	10 p.m.	A, B, C, Coys were all employed upon the clearance of C.T.s. 'D' Coy were distributed as follows ½ Platoon Light Railway, 1½ Platoons Dump, 2 Platoons T.M. emplacements. The following message was received from the O.R.2 "The A.D.M.S. 3rd Bri. tells me that the tram-lines were of great	P.J.

2449 Wt. W14957/Mgo 750,000 1/16 J.B.C. & A. Forms/C.2118/12.

WAR DIARY
or
INTELLIGENCE SUMMARY.
(Erase heading not required.)

Army Form C. 2118.

Place	Date	Hour	Summary of Events and Information	Remarks and references to Appendices
Courcelles	15/11/16	10p.m	value for removing wounded on the 13th and that necessary repairs were rapidly carried out by the party of Pioneers detailed for that purpose. Praise thanks those concerned." Lieut Penno was in charge of this party.	
Courcelles	16/11/16	10p.m	A, B, C, Coy carried on with the clearing and revetting of C.T's. D Coy carried on with work on Light Railway, T.M. emplacements and R.E. Dump	
Courcelles	17/11/16	10p.m	3 Platoons of A.B.C. Coy carried on with the clearing and revetting of C.T's in the Divisional Area. One platoon in each of these Coys rested. D. Coy carried on with work on Light Railway, T.M. emplacements. and R.E. Dump.	
Courcelles	18/11/16	10p.m	4 Platoon of A. Coy., 3 Platoons of B. Coy, and 4 Platoon of "D" Coy., continued their work on C.T's. 'D' Coy. had 1 Platoon on the Dump. 1½ Platoons on T.M. emplacements, and ½ Platoon on the Light Railway	
Courcelles	19/11/16	10p.m	A and C Coy continued working on the main C.T's in the Divisional Area. B Coy started work on clearing & revetting Monk Trench to make it into a V fire trench. D Coy carried on with work as before.	

Army Form C. 2118.

WAR DIARY
or
INTELLIGENCE SUMMARY.
(Erase heading not required.)

Instructions regarding War Diaries and Intelligence Summaries are contained in F. S. Regs., Part II. and the Staff Manual respectively. Title pages will be prepared in manuscript.

Place	Date	Hour	Summary of Events and Information	Remarks and references to Appendices
Courcelles	20/11/16	10 p.m.	"A" Coy. carried on with the drainage of Railway Av. between Rob Roy and Iron Line. "B" Coy. continued clearing and revetting Monk trench. "C" Coy. carried on with the clearing and revetting of Yellow Central, and Southern Avenues. "D" Coy. continued work on Dump, I.M. Emplacements, and Light Railway.	
Courcelles	21/11/16	10 p.m.	A, C, D, Coys. carried on with same work as for 20th inst. "B" Coy. started work on Brown Trench, just in front of Monk, clearing and constructing fire-bays and traverses.	
Courcelles	22/11/16	10 p.m.	The whole form companies carried on with the same work as for 21st inst., with the exception of 1 Platoon "D" Coy. who started on Divisional School Hdqrs.	
Courcelles	23/11/16	10 p.m.	B and C Coys. worked on C.T's, A Coy rested, D Coy carried on with same work as for 22nd inst.	
Courcelles	24/11/16	10 p.m.	"B" Coy. worked on C.T's, "D" Coy on Dump, T.M. emplacements and huts at Vauchelles, "A" and "C" Coys were held in readiness to start moving the Yellow Line.	
Courcelles	25/11/16	10 p.m.	During night 24-25 Novr. "A" and "C" Coys. commenced moving the Yellow Line. They moved M.G. positions 14 and 18 about 320 yds. in all. B.+D. carried on with usual work.	R.J.

Army Form C. 2118.

WAR DIARY
or
INTELLIGENCE SUMMARY

(Erase heading not required.)

Instructions regarding War Diaries and Intelligence Summaries are contained in F.S. Regs., Part II. and the Staff Manual respectively. Title Pages will be prepared in manuscript.

Place	Date	Hour	Summary of Events and Information	Remarks and references to Appendices
Courcelles	26/11/16	10 p.m.	During the night 25-26 Nov. A & C Coys started wiring Nos. 17 and 19 M.G. position. They completely wired about 520 yds. 'B' 'D' Coys carried on with manual work.	
Courcelles	27/11/16	10 p.m.	During the nights 26-27 Nov. A & C Coys completed the wiring of Nos. 17 and 19 M.G. positions and started wiring No. 21 M.G. position. They did about 550 yds. with the exception of 'B' 'D' Coys carried on with manual work on huts at the Dell.	
Courcelles	28/11/16	10 p.m.	1 Platoon B 'B' who started work on huts at the Dell. A and C Coys completed the wiring of M.G. positions Nos. 16 and 21. Putting up about 550 yds. of complete obstacle. Since Platoon of 'B' Coy worked on C.T's and one Platoon on huts at Bienvillers, one Platoon on C.T's as follows:— one Platoon on Light Railway, and one Platoon on carrying Dump, for 56th R.E.S. Party	
Courcelles	29/11/16	10 p.m.	A and C Coys completed the wiring of M.G. positions Nos. 14 and 20. Putting up about 500 yds. of complete obstacle. B and D Coys carried on with same work as for the 28th inst.	
Courcelles	30/11/16	6 p.m.	A Coy completed the wiring of M.G. positions 15 and C Coy the diagonal wire between M.G. positions 20 and 21, about 550 yds. in all. A letter from the G.O.C. 3rd Division stated that "the wiring of the Yellow Line was progressing very satisfactorily." B and D Coys carried on with the same work as for the 29th inst.	R. Syko Lt Col. Comdg 20 1/1cBn.

2449 Wt. W14957/Mgo 750,000 1/16 J.B.C. & A. Forms/C.2118/12.

War Diary Vol 1

20th (S) Battn. King's Royal Rifle Corps (Pioneers)

From 1st December 1916
To 31st December 1916

Volume IX

Army Form C. 2118.

WAR DIARY
or
INTELLIGENCE SUMMARY

(Erase heading not required.)

Instructions regarding War Diaries and Intelligence Summaries are contained in F. S. Regs., Part II. and the Staff Manual respectively. Title Pages will be prepared in manuscript.

Place	Date	Hour	Summary of Events and Information	Remarks and references to Appendices
Courcelles	1/12/16	10 p.m.	"A" & "C" Coys. rested with the exception that each Coy. sent a small party to thicken up the line in the Yellow Line by throwing in cross wire. "B" Coy. carried on with the work of clearing and revetting C.T's, and "D" Coy. made distributed as follows :— 1 Platoon & R.E. Dump, 1 Platoon on huts at Vauxhalles, 1½ Platoons carrying party for 56th R.E's, ½ Platoon on Light Railway.	
Courcelles	2/12/16	6 p.m.	"A" and "C" Coys. again rested with the exception of "D" Coy. carried on used for thickening the Yellow Line. "B" and "D" Coys. carried on as on the 1st. inst.	
Courcelles	3/12/16	6 p.m.	"A" & "C" Coys. continued wiring the "Yellow Line". "A" put up the second line for the No. 14 M.G. position, about 350 yds., while "C" put up 280 yds. "B" and diagonal lines between M.G. positions 20 and 21, about work as on the 2nd. inst. "D" Coy. carried on with same	
Courcelles	4/12/16	6 p.m.	"A" and "C" Coys. continued wiring the "Yellow Line". "A" constructed second line for M.G. position 15, distance about 350 yds., whilst "C" constructed second line for No. 20 M.G. position and about 100 yds. of second line for No. 21 M.G. position, total wire about 360 yds. "B" and "D" Coys. carried on with same work as for the 3rd. inst.	
Courcelles	5/12/16	6 p.m.	"A" and "C" Coys. continued wiring the "Yellow Line". "A" constructed diagonal between positions 14 and 15 and thickened up both positions. "C" Coy. constructed one third of obstacle round Basin Wood, and nearly completed No. 21 M.G. position. "B" and "D" Coys. carried on as for 4th. inst.	

2449 Wt. W14957/M90 750,000 1/16 J.B.C. & A. Forms/C.2118/12.

WAR DIARY
or
INTELLIGENCE SUMMARY

(Erase heading not required.)

Army Form C. 2118.

Place	Date	Hour	Summary of Events and Information	Remarks and references to Appendices
Courcelles	6/12/16	6 p.m.	'A' Coy. completed the wiring of M.G. position 17, first line, and constructed about one third of second line. 'C' Coy. completed wiring of M.G. position 21 and also the obstacle round Basin Wood. 'B' Coy. had three platoons working on C.T's, and one Platoon made road from Wanters - Euston Rd to Sackville Rd parallel for wheeled traffic. 'D' Coy. carried on as for the 5th inst.	
Courcelles	7/12/16	10 p.m.	'A' Coy. completed the wiring of the 2nd line of MT.G. E.17, about 200 yds. 'C' Coy. completed the wiring of the 2nd line of M.G. E.15, about 250 yds. 'B' Coy. continued work on C.T's and D. Coy. as for 6th inst.	
Courcelles	8/12/16	6 p.m.	'A' Coy. completed the wiring of M.G.E.16, about 200 yds. and 'C' Coy. B and D completed the wiring of No. 19 M.G.E. about 200 yds. Coys. carried on work as for the 7th inst.	
Courcelles	9/12/16	6 p.m.	A & C Coys. both worked with the exception that a small party from each Coy. fixed gutter line and 'A' in wire parties towards Euston. 'B' Coy. commenced the wire on our right covering the yellow line added to the divisional front. 'D' Coy. commenced work at 6 p.m. D. Coy. carried on with usual work.	

WAR DIARY
or
INTELLIGENCE SUMMARY.
(Erase heading not required.)

Army Form C. 2118.

Place	Date	Hour	Summary of Events and Information	Remarks and references to Appendices
Courcelles	10/12/16	6 p.m.	'B' Coy. moved the Yellow Line front obstacle from Cheero trench to the Serre Road – distance about 260 yds. 'D' Coy. carried on with their usual work. 'A' and 'C' Coys. rested.	
Courcelles	11/12/16	6 p.m.	'A' and 'C' Coys. wired the front of Baku trench from Jean Bart to Nairn St., a distance of about 500 yds. 'B' Coy continued Yellow Line to Borders Avenue – about 240 yds. 'D' Coy carried on as for the 10th inst.	
Courcelles	12/12/16	6 p.m.	A B C Coy. rested. 'D' Coy. carried on with usual work	
Courcelles	13/12/16	6 p.m.	Work for A, B, C Coys was cancelled by order of C.R.E. owing to fear of retaliation for our Artillery activity. 'D' Coy. carried on with usual work	
Courcelles	14/12/16	6 p.m.	'B' Coy. linked up the front line & wire of the Yellow Line with that of the 9th Div. about 260 yds. 'C' Coy. wired the second line of the Yellow Line from Cheero Trench to a point about 50 yds. N. of the Serre Rd., about 260 yds. 'A' Coy thickened the wire done by the 31st Div. from Jean Bart Railway to June Trench. 'D' Coy carried on with usual work.	C.J.

WAR DIARY
or
INTELLIGENCE SUMMARY.
(Erase heading not required.)

Army Form C. 2118.

Place	Date	Hour	Summary of Events and Information	Remarks and references to Appendices
Courcelles	15/12/16	6 p.m.	'A' Coy. thickened the second line of the Yellow Line were from the Batt Railway to Jena Trench "B" Coy completed the second line of the Yellow line was from a front about 5 yds N of Serre Row to Border Avenue, about 200 yds. "C" Coy thickened the front 35 line of the Yellow Line was from Light Railway (about 15 x 2) for a distance of about 300 yds. forwards. M.G. Emb. D. Coy carried on with usual work for 53rd Field Coy. R.E.	
Courcelles	16/12/16	6 p.m.	A Coy thickened the Second line of the Yellow line were from Railway to Jena Trench. B Coy placed Bombs in position and Salvaged Material. B. Thickened 2nd line were from Railway Avenue to M.G. 3. 14. C. Duck Boards on position and salvaged Material. D Co. Carried on usual work for 96. F.C. R.E	
Courcelles	17/12/16	6 p.m	A 13 HQ Coy Resting. D Co carried on usual work for 56th Fd Co. R E	

WAR DIARY
or
INTELLIGENCE SUMMARY.
(Erase heading not required.)

Army Form C. 2118.

Place	Date	Hour	Summary of Events and Information	Remarks and references to Appendices
Courcelles	18.12.16	6pm	A Coy clearing & repairing main C.T.s. and completing diversion not in course. B Coy. clearing, draining and repairing main C.T.s. C Coy & D Coy toleaving repairing main C.T.s. ½ Coy repairing road & telamp to Hebuterne.	
Courcelles	19.12.16	6pm	D Coy continued usual work for 56th Co R.E. A, B + C Coy continued work on clearing & revetting C.T.s D Coy continued usual work for 56th yds Co. R.E.	
Courcelles	20.11.16	6pm	A, B + C Coy continued on Clearing revetting C.T.s D Coy continued usual work for 56th yds Co R.E.	
Courcelles	21.12.16	6pm	A B + C Coy continued work on C.T.s D Coy continued work for 56th ½ Co R.E.	
Courcelles	22.11.16	4pm	A B + C Coy continued work on draining C.T. D Coy continued work for 56th yds Co R.E.	
Courcelles	23.12.16	6pm	A B + C Coy continued work on clearing & revetting and repairing and laying track Boards. D Coy Continued work for 56 & Co R.E	

WAR DIARY
or
INTELLIGENCE SUMMARY.
(Erase heading not required.)

Army Form C. 2118.

Place	Date	Hour	Summary of Events and Information	Remarks and references to Appendices
Courcelles	24/12/16	6 pm	A B + C Coy continued work on main C T's. R Coy continued work for 56 Fd Co R E	
Courcelles	25/12/16	6 pm	Party from B Coy pumping water from German Railway Dugouts at Reservoir of Battle Wood to dustman Say.	
Courcelles	26/12/16	6 pm	A B + C Coy continued work on main C T. D Coy continued work for 56 Fd Co R E	
Courcelles	27/12/16	6 pm	A B + C Coy continued work on main C T. D Coy continued work for 56 Fd Co R E	
Bruxelles	28/12/16	6 pm	A B + C Coy continued work on main C T. D Coy continued work for 56 Fd Co R E	
Courcelles	29/12/16	6 pm	A B + C Coy continued work on main C T. D Coy continued work for 56 Fd Co R E	
Courcelles	30/12/16	6 pm	A B + C Coy continued work on main C T's. D Coy continued work for 56th C R E	
Courcelles	31/12/16	6 pm	A. B. C. Coys continued work on the main C T's. D Coy continued work for 50th Div dated by R E.	R. Asken Lt Col (Ing) 20 KOYLI

3RD DIVISION — 1917
76TH INF. BDE

B. H. Q.
2ND SUFFOLKS.
8TH K.O.ROY. LANCS.
10TH R. WELCH FUS.
1ST GORDON HRS.
76TH MACHINE GUN COY.